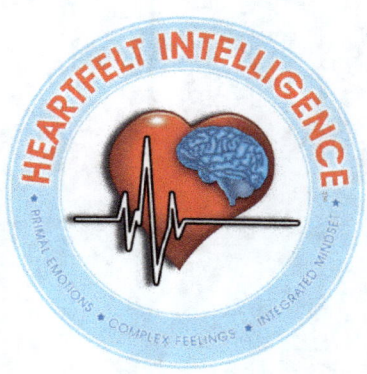

I dedicate this book to Mr. Robert (Bob) Jerus.

He is my Emotional Intelligence mentor, coach, and friend.

TABLE OF CONTENTS

HEARTfelt Emotions: Unleashing the Strength Within

"But the fruit of the Spirit is love, joy, peace, forbearance, kindness, goodness, faithfulness, gentleness, and self-control. Against such things there is no law." - Galatians 5:22-23 (NIV)

EMBODIED IN US IS A pool of fervent feelings. A celebration of life, expressed by our beating hearts and spirited souls. Each day, our joys and sorrows artfully paint our unique human journey.

Love, joy, and gratitude light our path, accompanied by empathy and kindness, our steadfast guides. Together, they form the agile keys that unlock our human grace, guiding us to a realm of radiance.

Yet, life can cloud our perceptions with pain and fear, hindering our understanding of reality. When faced with these dark clouds, we must delve into the depths of our beings to find the beacon that will guide us towards clarity.

Embedded in our HEARTfelt Emotions is a powerful cipher capable of crafting a life of joy and liberation. Let us honor this emotional tapestry as the powerful catalyst it is, capable of liberating our spirits.

By cherishing our individuality and unique personality, we remain authentic to our essence. This sincerity carves out paths towards joy and enigmatic riches of emotion.

Our wellbeing must remain our priority, demanding our respect and care for our bodies and minds. By loving and caring for ourselves, we elevate our emotional existence.

Momentum acts as the invincible force that propels us forward, helping us triumph over life's myriad challenges. Let's harness this potent energy to illuminate our lives.

When met with adversity, diminishment, or pain, let's recall the truth that resilience is within our reach. The Law of Change serves as a timely reminder that even in darkest hours, our inner strength prevails.

The influence of Contagion, an unseen force, pervades our surroundings – it can either raise us or pull us down. Our choice should always be to dispense love and light, crafting a world flourishing in kindness and brilliance.

Let's cherish the moment at hand, for it's within the present that our extraordinary tales unravel. Value each moment, for it's within these fragments of time that we find our story.

NAVIGATING FAITH AND PRINCIPLES: A NOTE TO READERS

In crafting this book, it is important to note that while biblical scriptures are referenced and woven into the narrative, the intention is not to impose a specific religious belief or dictate a particular way of life. The inclusion of these scriptures serves as a source of inspiration and wisdom, providing valuable insights into the principles of emotional intelligence.

The author recognizes the diverse backgrounds and beliefs of readers and encourages an open-minded exploration of the material. It is emphasized that the application of the 16 Laws of HEARTfelt Emotions is not contingent on adopting a particular faith or lifestyle. Instead, the goal is to present universal principles that transcend religious boundaries, promoting emotional well-being and fulfillment for individuals from all walks of life.

The author personally lives by these principles and finds resonance with the teachings in biblical scriptures. However, the book encourages readers to interpret and apply the content in a way that aligns with their own belief systems and values. The intent is to create a space for self-reflection, personal growth, and the development of emotional intelligence, irrespective of religious affiliations. The journey outlined in these pages is one of self-discovery, understanding, and transformation, allowing readers to draw inspiration from diverse sources and make the teachings their own.

"Emotional Intelligence is the ability to perceive emotions, to access and generate emotions so as to assist thought, to understand emotions and emotional knowledge, and to reflectively regulate emotions so as to promote emotional and intellectual growth." - Mayer & Salovey, 1997

PREFACE

"Everyone should be quick to listen, slow to speak and slow to become angry, because human anger does not produce the righteousness that God desires." - James 1:19-20 (NIV)

HEARTfelt Intelligence: More Than Just Emotional Intelligence

AT HEARTFELT INTELLIGENCE, WE FIRMLY believe that emotional intelligence forms a crucial pillar of both personal triumph and career prosperity. But, acknowledging this, we also comprehend that a profound layer of emotional intelligence transcends basic cognition and intellectual capabilities. This realization truly embodies what HEARTfelt Intelligence stands for.

Seeding from this understanding, our approach takes a unique trajectory aimed at "heartfelt intelligence." Our focus is on the intricate and deeply rooted connection between the heart and the mind. Science backs this connection - ample research illuminates the strong interconnectivity between our heart and brain. It delves deeper to reveal that the coherence of emotions between these two core elements can catalyze enhanced cognitive efficiency, emotional control, and an enriched sense of wellbeing.

We, at HEARTfelt Intelligence, are dedicated to aiding individuals and organizations in cultivating this fusion of the heart and mind. Our diverse array of programs and services are meticulously designed not only to elevate emotional self-awareness, empathy, and social abilities but to lay certain emphasis on the significance of heart coherence as well. As proponents of heartfelt intelligence, we religiously believe that its cultivation can empower individuals to unlock higher levels of personal fulfillment and success, and in the process, bumper positive impacts in the world they navigate through.

Boasting a team of diversified professionals, we amalgamate a diverse set of skills and experience drawn from psychology, education, and business. Our vigor drives us to assist people to unravel their full potential by harnessing their heartfelt intelligence.

We extend a warm invitation for you to delve into our broad variety of programs and services, ushering you to embark on this journey with us towards a novel, more heart-centered approach to emotional intelligence.

TRANSCENDING THE BOUNDS OF EMOTIONAL INTELLIGENCE

In the realm of emotional intelligence, the intricate interconnectedness of our heart and brain is of imperative significance. Emotional intelligence encapsulates the capacity to identify, comprehend, manage our own emotions, and empathize with the emotions of others. This intricate process is not confined to cognitive abilities but extends into the physiological sphere as well.

Numerous scientific studies affirm that the heart and brain, through the nervous system, possess an intricate relationship. Intriguingly, the heart has its own elaborate nervous system named the autonomic nervous system, which communicates with the brain via the vagus nerve. This channel of communication is bidirectional - the heart has the capability to relay information to the brain and vice versa.

An exemplification of this connection manifests in the form of "emotional coherence." This phenomenon arises when there's a synchronization between heart rate variability and brain waves activity. The state of emotional coherence is related to enhancements in cognitive performance, the ability to regulate emotions, and an improvement in overall well-being.

Therefore, in the context of emotional intelligence, developing the ability to regulate our own emotions can yield positive impacts on both the heart and brain. It promotes a state of emotional coherence, contributing to the enhancement of overall health and well-being. Unfortunately, any relevant answer beyond this would require additional information not provided in the document data.

HEARTfelt Emotions: A Profound Inner Resonance

HEARTfelt emotions are deep-rooted emotions, the ones that profoundly resonate within us - so deeply that they touch the innermost layers of our souls. These raw, unfiltered emotions seep in when we relate with something or someone at an intensely profound level; when a connection beyond the ordinary is forged.

Experiencing these emotions often leaves us feeling vulnerable and exposed, as if our innermost selves are put on display for the world to see. Despite this exposure, it is within this expression that a cathartic sense of liberation and release is found.

Heartfelt emotions are diverse, donning various forms. They could be the overwhelming surge of joy that courses through us on witnessing awe-inspiring beauty, the heartache that accompanies the loss of a loved one, or the intense passion ignited within us for a cause or an idea.

Regardless of their form, heartfelt emotions wield the power to stir us, to effect deep personal transformations. They bestow upon us a kind of connection with the world around us that goes beyond the ordinary. This connection is deeply transformative and meaningful, imbuing our lives with a sense of purpose that transcends the mundane.

So, if you ever find yourself at a crossroads unsure of your course, listen to your heartfelt emotions. Trust your heart's power. Let the world's beauty and wonder move and inspire you. You may be pleasantly surprised; extraordinary things might unfold when you let your HEARTfelt emotions guide you.

PRIMAL EMOTIONS: THE FOUNDATION OF OUR EMOTIONAL MAKEUP

Primal emotions are our core instinctive emotional responses, hardwired into our human consciousness, often associated with basic survival instincts. These emotions include fear, anger, joy, sadness, and surprise. Universally experienced across cultures, primal emotions serve as a unifying thread within the human experience.

An example that vividly paints the role of primal emotions would be the universally felt emotion of fear. Let's consider a scenario where an unknown, unanticipated sound is heard late at night. The rush of fear is immediate and involuntary, an instinctual response to a potential threat. Your heart rate increases, adrenaline surges, and attention sharpens. These physiological changes prepare you to either confront or escape the potential danger—an instinct for survival hardwired in every human across cultures, placing it squarely within primal emotions.

Primal emotions, with their universal, fundamental nature, form the building blocks of our emotional repertoire. They act as the foundational layer upon which complex emotions, cultural nuances, and individual emotional intelligence grow and evolve. Although these emotions may be instinctive, understanding and navigating them remains a profound aspect of our human experience.

From the document data provided, a more detailed progression into this topic might prove challenging. However, the existing content establishes a clear understanding of primal emotions, their universality, and how they are fundamentally connected to our survival instincts.

COMPLEX EMOTIONS: HIGHER-LEVEL EMOTIONS INTERWOVEN WITH CULTURE AND LEARNING

In contrast to primal emotions, complex emotions unfold on a higher plane, demanding social and cultural learning experiences for their evolvement. The palette of these sophisticated emotions includes emotive states like guilt, shame, envy, pride, and empathy, to enumerate a few.

Unlike primal emotions recognized irrespective of cultural background, complex emotions are intrinsically linked to diversely varying contexts of sociocultural environs. They do not uphold the universal constants of primal emotions; instead, their interpretation fluctuates across diverse cultures.

One exemplary rendition of a complex emotion would be guilt. This emotion materializes when one believes (rightly or wrongly) that they have violated a moral standard. It largely depends on moral codes which could vary considerably across different societies and cultures.

These comparisons illuminate the layered complexities of emotions, showcasing the dynamic interplay between instinctive emotional responses and those refined by cultural and societal nuances. Accordingly, an extensive understanding and management of both primal and complex emotions can equip individuals with an integrated mindset, allowing for practical emotional intelligence.

INTEGRATED MINDSET: A HARMONIOUS BLEND OF EMOTIONS FOR PERSONAL GROWTH

Possessing an integrated mindset signifies the ability to harmoniously regulate and balance both instinctive, primal emotions and socially learned, complex emotions. This equilibrium promotes a sense of well-being and contributes to personal growth. The embodiment of an integrated mindset involves self-awareness; recognizing and understanding one's own emotional responses, and subsequently using this understanding to make adaptive choices intentionally.

An integrated mindset serves as a tool, aiding individuals in managing stress, fostering positive relationships, and actualizing their goals. A crucial facet of this mindset is the development of emotional intelligence, which is the discerning ability to identify, comprehend, and govern our own emotions and empathize with the emotions of others.

Take the example of a workplace scenario - an individual with an integrated mindset is confronted with a conflict. They might initially feel the primal emotion of anger. However, instead of reacting impulsively driven by this anger, their integrated mindset kicks in. They reflect upon their complex emotions of empathy and understanding, leading them to engage in a constructive dialogue and resolve the conflict amicably.

This conscious modulation of primal and complex emotions exemplifies the potential of an integrated mindset in promoting personal growth, healthy relationships, and well-being, thus transforming both their personal and professional lives.

"In the harmony of heart and mind, within the dance of primal and complex emotions, we unlock the rhythm of an integrated mindset. It is here that we find our strength, harnessing the momentum to transcend, to transform adversity into prosperity, and illuminate our world with love, light, and heartfelt intelligence." – Dr. Tracie Hines Lashley

"From the primal depths of our hearts to the complex landscapes of our minds, lies the orchestration of our emotional symphony. Embrace this dance of feelings, for it is in this rhythm, that life finds its most heartfelt melody." – Robert (Bob) Jerus

ACKNOWLEDGEMENTS

HEARTFELT THANKS TO OUR ESTEEMED REVIEWERS

AS WE STAND ON THE threshold of launching "16 Laws of HEARTfelt Emotions - The Power of Emotional Awareness to THRIVE," we pause to express our deepest gratitude to the incredible individuals who lent their time, insights, and hearts to review this book.

Your contributions have been more than just reviews; they have been acts of collaboration, infusing this journey with diverse perspectives and wisdom. Each page now bears the imprint of your understanding and empathy, enriching the tapestry of emotional intelligence that we have strived to weave.

To those who pored over the chapters, offering constructive feedback, challenging our thoughts, and sharing your emotional narratives - your input has been invaluable. You have not only helped shape this book but have also touched our lives profoundly, reminding us of the power of collective growth and understanding.

Your dedication, honesty, and passion have been instrumental in bringing this project to fruition. This book, now ready to make its way into the world, is a testament to your belief in the transformative power of emotional awareness.

As we share "16 Laws of HEARTfelt Emotions" with readers worldwide, we carry with us the gratitude for your invaluable contributions. Thank you for joining us on this journey and for helping us nurture a world more in tune with its emotions, one reader at a time.

With heartfelt appreciation,

Dr. Tracie Hines Lashley

- **Mr. Robert (Bob) Jerus**
- **Mrs. Valinda Russell Jackson**
- **Mr. Myron Keith Hines**
- **Ms. Kayla Tobin**
- **Mrs. Crystal Voiles**
- **Mrs. Lilian Okech**

DISCOVER THE IMPACT OF "16 LAWS OF HEARTFELT EMOTIONS" THROUGH THE VOICES OF OUR READERS

Interested in learning how "16 Laws of HEARTfelt Emotions - The Power of Emotional Awareness to THRIVE" has touched the lives of others? Visit our website to explore a collection of heartfelt testimonials from readers who have embarked on this transformative journey. Their experiences and insights offer a glimpse into the profound impact this book has had on personal growth and emotional understanding. Join the community of readers and see how this book could resonate with your own journey towards emotional intelligence.

Visit www.heartfelteiq.com for testimonials and more information.

"Emotions are not a luxury item, they are a crucial element to our well-being." - Dalai Lama

INTRODUCTION

"Create in me a pure heart, O God, and renew a steadfast spirit within me." - Psalm 51:10 (NIV)

"Above all else, guard your heart, for everything you do flows from it." - Proverbs 4:23 (NIV)

"And now these three remain: faith, hope, and love. But the greatest of these is love." - 1 Corinthians 13:13 (NIV)

CHRIST-CENTERED

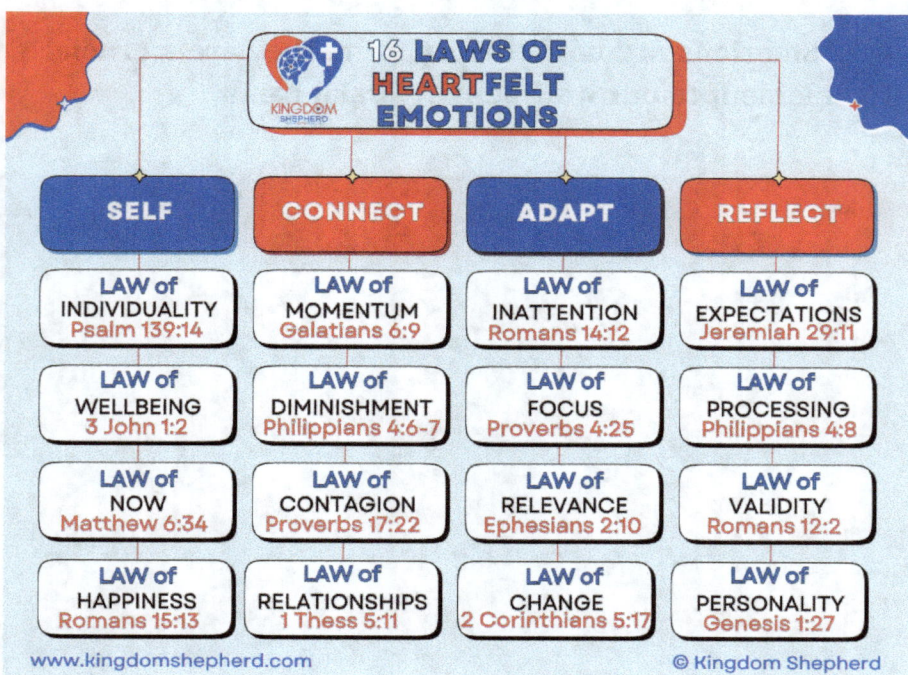

STANDARD

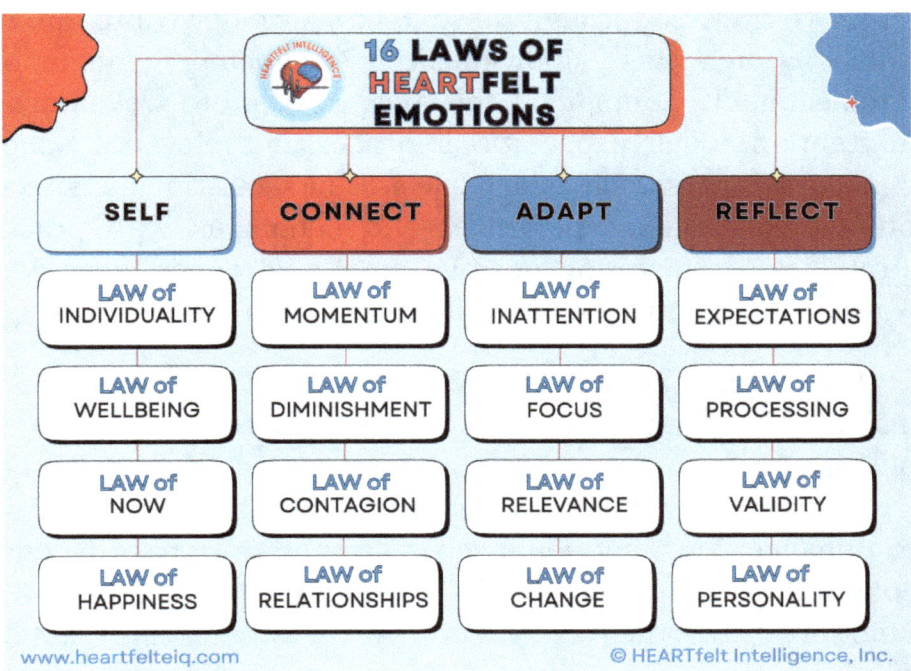

EMOTIONS, IN ALL THEIR HUES and shades, deeply sculpt the essence of our human experience. They influence our relationships, direct our decisions, and enrich our general sense of wellness and wholeness. However, the path of emotions can often be a labyrinth – teeming with confusion and laden with the weight of overwhelming experiences. The echo of our emotions can likely resonate with feelings of perturbation and trepidation.

With "The 16 Laws of HEARTfelt Emotions," we aim to demystify this labyrinth – sketching a series of guiding principles to offer clarity and aid in the understanding and nurturing of our emotional landscape. Each law, grounded in meticulous research and psychological theory, acts as a beacon leading to emotional wellbeing and fulfillment.

As we traverse through these 16 Laws, we delve into different arenas such as individuality, wellbeing, momentum, diminishment, contagion, the power of now, relationships, inattention, focus, expectations, processing, relevance, validity, change, and personality. Each law presents a distinct perspective on our emotional experiences and equips us with practical strategies for fostering positive emotional experiences whilst warding off negative emotional entanglement.

This book is curated for every individual who seeks deeper insight into their emotional journey and craves a practical blueprint towards emotional wellness and fulfillment. Irrespective of whether you're battling negative emotions, wish to enhance your emotional self-awareness, or yearn to enrich your life with more joy and fulfillment, "The 16 Laws of HEARTfelt Emotions" paves the way for a positive and wholesome emotional existence.

By assimilating these transformative laws, we gain profound insight into our emotional experiences, laying a solid foundation for substantial emotional wellbeing and fulfillment. So, let's embark on this journey of emotional growth with the 16 Laws of HEARTfelt Emotions.

INTRODUCING THE INSPIRATIONAL AUNT GRACE

Imbued with deep wisdom, compassion, and warmth, Aunt Grace is a beacon of emotional intelligence. Her humble beginnings in a small town, where she shouldered the responsibility of caring for her younger siblings and extended family, shaped her empathetic and nurturing spirit. It is this innate ability to form deep connections and provide support that steered her towards a fulfilling career in counseling and social work.

Throughout her career, Aunt Grace had the privilege to work with myriad individuals and families. Her empathetic ear and understanding heart guided them through life's demanding labyrinth. Gifted in active listening and deeply attuned to the complexities of human experiences, she stands as a pillar of support and guidance to all who have crossed paths with her.

In her personal sphere, Aunt Grace is revered for her kind-heartedness and generous spirit. A devoted wife, mother, and grandmother, she has made her home a sanctuary of warmth, welcoming everyone with open arms. Her gentle yet formidable persona and quiet resilience inspire those around her to strive for their best.

Although Aunt Grace's own journey was not devoid of adversities, she faced life's challenges with remarkable grace and resilience. These experiences provided her with valuable insights into the importance of emotional intelligence and the power of deep self-connection.

Now in the golden years of her life, Aunt Grace has pledged herself to impart the wisdom she has gleaned over the years and assist others in unveiling the transformative magic of emotional intelligence. She seeks to guide others towards a fulfilling and authentic life, fostering a deep connection with their hearts and the world around them.

One scripture that mirrors Aunt Grace's life principles is from 1 Corinthians 13:4-7 "Love is patient, love is kind. It does not envy, it does not boast, it is not proud. It does not dishonor others, it is not self-seeking, it is not easily angered, it keeps no record of wrongs. Love does not delight in evil but rejoices with the truth. It always protects, always trusts, always hopes, always perseveres."

These words encapsulate values Aunt Grace cherishes and practices - patience, kindness, humility, respect for others, forgiveness, and perseverance. Her life is a testament to these values, enabling her to establish profound relationships and serve as a beacon of hope and encouragement to her community.

Integrating these principles of love and compassion into her existence, Aunt Grace has managed to craft a life brimming with joy, purpose, and emotional intelligence. Moreover, she inspires others to embark on a similar path.

Aunt Grace shines as a living example of how the 16 Laws of HEARTfelt Emotions can transform everyday life. Throughout the pages of this book, she shares enlightening anecdotes and examples drawn from her experiences, as well as from others. These illustrate how the Laws can assist in overcoming hurdles, nurturing deep bonds, and cultivating a purposeful life.

Numerous individuals and families have benefited from Aunt Grace's wisdom and insights, maneuvering the intricacies of their emotional lives with her guidance. Her indefatigable passion for emotional intelligence is palpable in all her endeavors.

As we delve into Grace's narratives about various life principles, we specifically situate her in distinct parts of her house based on the theme of the discussions.

When the conversation turns towards **self-awareness**, Grace finds herself in the _kitchen_, a symbolic place of nurturing and intake, mirroring the idea of internal reflections and self-growth.

The _family room_, where **relationships** get nurtured, becomes the setting when Grace discusses relationships, capturing the essence of bonding and emotional closeness.

The _garden_, a serene spot representative of cultivation and growth, serves as the backdrop when topics veer towards **self-management**, echoing our personal efforts to grow and develop.

Lastly, when discussions move towards **social awareness and empathy**, Grace transitions to the _porch_. The porch, a bridge between personal and outside world, symbolizes how we perceive and interact with the wider social fabric, just as we engage with the broader world from our enclosed porch.

This spatial alignment enhances Grace's stories, enabling each location to complement the emotions and wisdom visually and symbolically she shares.

With Aunt Grace serving as our guide, we can uncover the transformative essence of the 16 Laws of HEARTfelt Emotions. Together, we can realize the joy and connection that sprouts from living with an open heart and a profound sense of purpose.

CHAPTER SUMMARY

This chapter lays the foundation for the book "The 16 Laws of HEARTfelt Emotions," and introduces readers to the idea that emotions, whether positive or negative, significantly shape our lives and our experiences of it. The book aims to guide readers in understanding and managing these emotions, and underlines that its laws are applicable to anyone seeking to cultivate emotional wellness and enhance their self-awareness.

This introductory chapter also presents Aunt Grace, a key guide throughout this emotional journey. She embodies the perfect amalgamation of wisdom, compassion, and warmth, and epitomizes the practice of the 16 Laws. Aunt Grace's insights, drawn from her experiences as a counselor, social worker, and through her personal life struggles, form the cornerstone of this journey towards emotional intelligence.

The book illustrates the importance of values such as patience, kindness, humility, respect for others, forgiveness, and perseverance, all of which Aunt Grace embodies in her life and work. Through these principles, the book aims to help individuals create a purposeful life filled with joy, emotional intelligence, and deep connections. The readers are invited to join this journey, with Aunt Grace as their guide, to uncover the transformative essence of the 16 Laws of HEARTfelt Emotions and to bask in the joy and connection that stems from living with an open heart and profound sense of purpose.

APPLICATION

Implementing the knowledge, we acquire is a crucial step on the path to personal and professional growth. Merely gaining knowledge isn't enough, it must be put into action in pragmatic ways to garner concrete results and make progress towards our goals. By harnessing new knowledge, we can refine our skills, build confidence, and edge closer to success.

Here are some ways to apply the knowledge gained in everyday life:

1. **Seek Self-Relevance:** Begin a journal to note down your thoughts and feelings. This simple act can lead to more profound self-understanding and relevance of your emotions.

2. **Practice Mindfulness:** Attempt a mindfulness practice such as a body-scan or breathing exercise. It can help enhance emotional regulation and stress management.

3. **Foster Relationships:** Write a letter or message to someone you appreciate. Active recognition of valuable relationships in our life can further enrich our emotional well-being.

4. **Stay Present:** Practice being present in the moment - during a conversation, meal, or any activity. Presence enhances the connection with our emotional state and surroundings, leading to better emotional health.

5. **Manage Emotional Disposition:** Take a break from technology and spend time in nature or engage in a hobby you enjoy. Such activities can help avoid negative emotions and promote emotional disposition.

6. **Develop Expectation Management:** Visualize yourself successfully completing a task. This helps in managing expectations and contributes to a positive experience of emotions.

Remember, the journey to emotional wellbeing is progressive, not instant. By meticulously and consistently implementing these steps, we can create a fulfilling emotional life, promoting overall health and happiness.

"Life is a journey, and if you fall in love with the journey, you will be in love forever." - Peter Hagerty

THE JOURNEY TO SELF-AWARENESS & WELLBEING

"May the God of hope fill you with all joy and peace as you trust in him, so that you may overflow with hope by the power of the Holy Spirit." - Romans 15:13 (NIV)

"Be yourself; everyone else is already taken." - Oscar Wilde

THE LAW OF INDIVIDUALITY

"I praise you because I am fearfully and wonderfully made; your works are wonderful; I know that full well."
- Psalm 139:14 (NIV)

THE PRINCIPLE OF INDIVIDUALITY REVOLVES around the unique and individualized nature of our emotional experiences. Each person's emotions are intricately shaped by their personal history, beliefs, and experiences, creating a unique emotional blueprint that deserves respect and validation.

Emotions, deeply personal and subjective, are inherently shaped by our distinctive histories, beliefs, and experiences. The Law of Individuality firmly acknowledges the validity of everyone's emotional experiences. It underscores the fundamental right we all have for our emotional experiences to be respected and validated.

While there might be some shared semblance in the emotional experiences between individuals, it is essential to note that no two people undergo the same emotional journey. Our emotions are seen through the lens of individual perspectives, values, and beliefs, embodying a deep level of personal uniqueness.

The Law of Individuality serves as a reminder that our emotional experiences form an integral part of our authentic selves. Denying or repressing our emotions equates to denying a part of our very existence. It then becomes intrinsic to acknowledge and express our emotions in a healthful and constructive manner, honoring our individuality and advocating for emotional wellbeing.

However, the unique nature of each emotional experience can often create hurdles in connecting with others, fostering feelings of misunderstanding, loneliness, or isolation. To mitigate these challenges, the cultivation of empathy and understanding becomes vital.

In practical terms, this cultivation could involve seeking out supportive communities of individuals undergoing similar emotional experiences. It could also entail engaging in honest and transparent communication with loved ones regarding our emotions. Curiosity and openness towards understanding others' emotional journeys and validating their unique perspectives are equally crucial.

By embracing and adhering to The Law of Individuality, we afford ourselves the potential to foster a deeper understanding and appreciation of our own emotional experiences. It enables us to nourish our relationships, instilling them with compassion and strength.

A STORY FROM GRACE'S KITCHEN: THE LAW OF INDIVIDUALITY

On a calm evening, Aunt Grace was found in her comforting kitchen, baking cookies with the delightful aroma wafting through the house. Her kitchen, symbolizing the heart of the house, often served as the breeding ground for profound lessons on self-awareness that she dispensed as lovingly as she did the food.

Her nieces and nephews, drawn by the smell of freshly baked cookies, sauntered in. Seeing this as an opportunity, Aunt Grace smiled wisely and began to teach them about the Law of Individuality.

"You know, dear ones," Aunt Grace began, "Each of you will leave a distinct handprint on the cookie dough, and no two prints will be the same. This is just like our emotions. Although we have similar feelings sometimes, each of us experiences them differently. Each person's emotions are intricately shaped by their personal history, beliefs, and experiences." As she let this thought settle, she keenly observed their reactions.

The children, with furrowed brows, slowly began to understand this concept.

"And remember," she continued, "These unique emotional experiences are what make you who you are. They are precious and deserve respect, just as you do."

Aunt Grace's inspirational speech about the Law of Individuality taught them a valuable lesson that day - that their uniqueness is not just about their physical attributes or talents, but also about their emotional experiences. Her teachings, held in the heart of her home, the kitchen, served to underscore the tenets of self-awareness and the value of the individual experience. In doing so, Aunt Grace manifested her mission of helping others discover the transformative power of emotional intelligence once again.

Thus, a regular day in Aunt Grace's kitchen was turned into an enriching learning experience that the children would remember and apply in their lives.

CHAPTER SUMMARY

In the chapter on The Law of Individuality, the fundamental significance of individual emotional experiences in shaping one's identity is explored.

The scripture verse that emphasizes this chapter is Psalm 139:14 (NIV): "I praise you because I am fearfully and wonderfully made; your works are wonderful; I know that full well."

Individuality pertains to the deeply personal and unique nature of our emotional experiences, which are molded by personal history, beliefs, and experiences. Each individual's emotional encounters are validated and respected, appreciating their pivotal contribution to our individual uniqueness.

While there may be shared emotional experiences among individuals, the rule emphasizes that no two people experience emotions identically. Emotions are filtered through individual perspectives, values, and beliefs, which render them deeply personal and unique. It propounds that our emotional experiences are an authentic and vital manifestation of our individual selves, and suppression or denial of these equates to denying a part of our identity.

The chapter also acknowledges the challenges of individual emotional experiences, such as the difficulty in connecting with others or feeling isolated. It proposes empathetic understanding and validation of others' emotional experiences as the solution.

The chapter concludes with practical initiatives to celebrate the Law of Individuality, suggesting activities to embrace your uniqueness and foster emotional wellbeing. Following the Law of Individuality allows for a deeper understanding of our emotional experiences, paving the way for compassionate relationships with others.

APPLICATION

Applying the knowledge, we have gathered is instrumental in achieving personal and professional growth. Knowledge attainment alone is insufficient; it must be translated into pragmatic actions to yield tangible outcomes and progress towards our aspirations. By putting our newfound knowledge into practice, we're able to refine our skills, enhance our confidence, and advance towards success.

To apply the knowledge, you've gained from this chapter on the Law of Individuality, here are some helpful steps:

1. **Embrace Your Uniqueness:** Write down three aspects that make you unique and celebrate them, acknowledging your individual value adds to your emotional wellbeing.

2. **Explore New Experiences:** Try a new hobby or activity that has piqued your interest in the past.

3. **Visualize Your Passions:** Create a vision board that symbolizes your unique passions and interests to have a clear picture of your intrinsic values and desires.

4. **Align with Your Values:** Identify your personal values and evaluate how you can better align your everyday actions and decisions with these values.

5. **Reflect on Your Desires:** Spend some quiet time alone to reflect on your innermost desires and dreams, a practice that can lead to better self-understanding and emotional alignment.

These steps serve as a practical application of the Law of Individuality, reinforcing the importance of acknowledging and appreciating our personal experiences and emotions as unique and sculptors of our identity.

"The greatest wealth is health." - Virgil

THE LAW OF WELLBEING

"Dear friend, I pray that you may enjoy good health and that all may go well with you, even as your soul is getting along well." - 3 John 1:2 (NIV)

THE PRECEPT OF WELLBEING UNDERSCORES the utmost importance of emotional health, both in the pursuit of holistic health and happiness. It encapsulates various factors such as efficiently managing stress and emotional regulation, along with ensuring reliable social support. Preserving this blend is crucial to leading a fulfilling and enriching life.

Emotional well-being, pivotal to total health and happiness, is at the forefront of the Law of Wellbeing. This law fosters the import of emotional wellness and imparts crucial guidance for nurturing a life abundant in positive and fulfilling emotions.

The journey towards emotional wellbeing comprises intricate aspects, including stress management, emotional regulation, as well as having appropriate social support. Overlooking our emotional wellbeing can lead to detrimental consequences, such as heightened stress, difficulties in emotion regulation, and a reduced quality of life.

To champion emotional wellbeing, it's vital to give precedence to both self-care and emotional cognizance. This could entail integrating practices like mindfulness, meditation, or physical exercise into our routine, in addition to seeking support from mental health specialists or those we hold dear.

Simultaneously, it's essential to nurture emotional regulation skills, including the ability to identify and express emotions in a healthy, constructive manner. By mastering the regulation of our emotions, we propel ourselves towards better handling stress and anxiety, thereby building a potent and more upbeat emotional life.

Furthermore, fostering social support is intrinsic to emotional wellbeing. Cultivating vigorous and wholesome relationships with friends, family, and within our community can instill a sense of belonging and emotional support. This, in turn, serves to encourage positive emotional experiences.

In application, this could involve participation in community groups or clubs, surrounding oneself with supportive friends or family members, or partaking in activities that enhance social connection.

By honoring the Law of Wellbeing, we pave the way towards a robust and upbeat emotional life, laying the groundwork for enhanced health and happiness.

A STORY FROM GRACE'S GARDEN: THE LAW OF WELLBEING

On a serene afternoon, you would find Aunt Grace in her plush garden, a sanctuary of tranquil self-management, where age-old trees whispered tales of wisdom, and each blooming flower echoed her philosophy of emotional wellbeing.

Surrounded by vibrant blooms, Aunt Grace was found assisting her youngest grandchild in planting a seedling. A question sparkled in the child's eyes, "Why do we need to water this little seed, Grandma?"

Smiling at the child's curiosity, Aunt Grace ingeniously transformed the simple gardening act into a profound lesson on the Law of Wellbeing.

"Just like this tiny seed requires sunlight, water, and care to bloom into a beautiful flower," she began, "our emotional wellbeing, too, needs nurturing. We must water it with self-awareness, let the sunlight of self-acceptance shine on it, and rid the soil around it of negativity."

"Our emotional wellbeing is a lot like this garden," she continued, pointing at the array of colorful flowers around them, "With care, it blooms into joy and fulfillment. Yet, if neglected, it can wither, just like these plants would." A glimpse at a wilted plant nearby made her point clearer.

"Our emotional garden demands us to manage stress, accept and regulate our emotions, and seek warmth and understanding from those around us," she explained further, tenderly watering the freshly sowed seedling.

As the child absorbed Aunt Grace's words, her garden seemed to buzz with newfound resonance. The blooms around them appeared to smile in confirmation of Aunt Grace's wisdom, mirroring the powerful lesson on the Law of Wellbeing.

That afternoon, the wisdom imparted amidst the blooming flowers left an indelible impact on the young mind. This story, shared from Aunt Grace's garden, held a life-long lesson for her grandchild, extending far beyond the realm of emotional wellbeing alone.

CHAPTER SUMMARY

The Law of Wellbeing is vital for overall health and happiness and plays a central role in achieving emotional wellness. The chapter illuminates the importance of stress management, emotional regulation, and social support as key constituents of emotional wellbeing.

The pivotal scripture underscoring this chapter is 3 John 1:2 (NIV): "Dear friend, I pray that you may enjoy good health and that all may go well with you, even as your soul is getting along well."

The chapter outlines that neglecting emotional wellbeing can lead to adverse outcomes such as heightened stress, difficulties in regulating emotions, and a decline in the quality of life. To foster emotional wellbeing, it is crucial to prioritize self-care, emotional awareness, and foster emotional regulation skills.

The chapter emphasizes the need for robust social support for maintaining emotional wellbeing. Building healthy relationships with friends, family, and community can provide a sense of belonging, emotional support, and promote positive emotional experiences.

Applying the Law of Wellbeing in life might entail integrating practices like mindfulness, meditation, or physical exercise. It could also involve seeking support from therapists or loved ones and developing a strong social support network.

The chapter concludes that honoring the Law of Wellbeing cultivates a positive emotional life, serving as a foundation for greater health and happiness. In-depth understanding and practice of this law can contribute to personal and professional growth and help individuals move closer to success.

APPLICATION

Implementing the knowledge, we've gathered into practical action plays a pivotal role in fostering personal and professional growth. Merely acquiring knowledge falls short; it must be executed in pragmatic ways to bear tangible results and inch closer to one's goals. Activating this newfound knowledge allows individuals to refine their skills, boost their confidence, and progress towards success.

Here are some steps to apply the principles of the Law of Wellbeing into your daily life:

1. **Cultivate Gratitude:** Start a daily gratitude practice. Acknowledge the good in your life, as this can shift your mindset towards a more positive outlook.

2. **Embrace Mindfulness:** Engage in a yoga class or mindfulness activity. These practices can create a sense of calm and help manage stress better.

3. **Prioritize Self-Care:** Create a morning routine that honors self-care. This could include practices such as stretching, meditation, or affirmations to set a positive tone for the rest of your day.

4. **Pursue Joy:** Make a list of activities that bring you joy and strive to incorporate them into your daily schedule. This can drastically improve your emotional wellbeing.

5. **Adopt a Healthy Lifestyle:** Try a new healthy habit, such as hydrating yourself more frequently or incorporating more

vegetables into your diet. Physical health profoundly impacts our emotional and overall wellbeing.

By faithfully integrating these steps into our daily routine, we honor the Law of Wellbeing, paving the path toward an emotionally rich and joyful life.

"Be present in all things and thankful for all things."
- Maya Angelou

THE LAW OF NOW

"Therefore, do not worry about tomorrow, for tomorrow will worry about itself. Each day has enough trouble of its own." - Matthew 6:34 (NIV)

THE DOCTRINE OF THE PRESENT, also known as The Law of NOW, enfolds a dominant principle - the essence of experiencing and processing our emotions is rooted deeply in the present moment. Prioritizing engagement and presence in our current encounters and situations enhance our emotional experience.

This law accentuates the vital role of existing in the moment for an enriching emotional life. The disregard of this law might turn us oblivious to fully experiencing our emotions, subsequently leading to amplified stress, regulation complexities, and a diminished sense of emotional wellbeing.

In honoring the Law of NOW, cultivating an awareness of the present moment and mindfulness is essential. This could be built by integrating practices such as meditation, deep breathing exercises or physical workouts into your daily routine, alongside seeking opportunities to engage in the present moment positively and constructively.

It is equally vital to deliberately engage and remain present in social interactions, work tasks, and all other activities we partake in daily. A heightened level of presence allows us to experience our emotions fully, thereby gaining a more profound understanding of our feelings and ourselves.

In a practical scenario, it might entail allocating time each day for mindful practices like deep breathing exercises or meditation. It could also suggest remaining fully engaged and present during social interactions, work tasks, and other pursuits, ensuring moments to pause and completely experience our emotions.

By honoring the Law of Now, we pave the path towards a deeper appreciation and understanding of our emotional experiences, laying the groundwork for a stable emotional wellbeing. Fully embracing the present moment endows us with the ability to thoroughly experience and process our emotions, contributing to a healthier and more fulfilling emotional life.

In conclusion, a brighter and more positive future awaits us by immersing ourselves fully in the present moment, as it's truly all we have. It holds the promise of a vibrant future not only for us but also those whose lives we touch.

STORY FROM GRACE'S PORCH: THE LAW OF NOW

In the calm dusk, you'd find Aunt Grace on her homely porch, a serene domain of social awareness and empathy, engaging in her evening pause. Overlooking her sunflower garden, a balmy breeze stirring the sunflower heads, Aunt Grace sat rocking in her favorite wooden chair, wrapped up in the tranquility of the moment.

Her young niece, visiting for the summer, joined her on the porch, a maze of worrisome thoughts unveiled on her innocent face. Aunt Grace sighed softly, turned to her and asked, "Tell me dear, what weighs on your mind?"

Confiding in Aunt Grace, the young girl shared her worries about tomorrow's school play. The anxious quest for a perfect performance worried her about unforeseen obstacles that might tarnish her efforts.

_Seeing the distress on her niece's face, Aunt Grace knew exactly what wisdom to share. "Do you see these sunflowers, dear?" she started, gesturing towards their golden heads swaying in the breeze, "They live in the NOW. They dance with the current wind, not worried about the winds that may come later."

"Our emotional wellbeing relies upon this principle– living in the present moment. The Law of Now reminds us to focus on the current moment, just as our sunflower friends. If we insist on worrying about tomorrow's wind, dear, we miss the present wind's dance." Aunt Grace bestowed her wisdom, her voice intertwined with the rustling leaves' chorus.

"Your school play is tomorrow, but your worries are for today. Focus on rehearsing and enjoying your part today. Let tomorrow arrive with its surprise." Grace pats her niece's hand, inspiring calm in her stormy thoughts.

That evening, Aunt Grace's porch transformed into an enlightening platform for understating The Law of NOW. The young girl's anxious thoughts subsided, replaced with a newfound mantra of embracing the present, fostering her emotional growth throughout the summer.

CHAPTER SUMMARY

The Law of NOW centralizes the importance of engaging fully in the present moment to experience and process our emotions completely. It emphasizes the significance of being present in our emotional experiences.

The key scripture guiding this chapter is Matthew 6:34 (NIV): "Therefore do not worry about tomorrow, for tomorrow will worry about itself. Each day has enough trouble of its own."

Failing to engage in the current moment might lead us to miss the full extent of our emotions, resulting in adverse effects like increased stress, difficulties in regulating emotions, and decreased emotional wellbeing.

To adhere to the Law of NOW, it's crucial to cultivate mindfulness and present-moment awareness. This can be achieved by integrating practices such as mindfulness meditation, deep breathing exercises, physical activity, and by seeking opportunities to engage with the present moment positively.

The chapter underscores the importance of being actively engaged and present in social interactions, work-based tasks, or any daily activities. Being fully engaged in the moment allows for a deepened experience of our emotions and fosters a better understanding of ourselves and our emotional experiences.

In practical terms, this could involve dedicating daily time for mindfulness exercises or ensuring full presence in everyday activities.

Honoring the Law of NOW leads us to a deeper appreciation of our emotional experiences and forms the foundation for enhanced emotional well-being. Remember, the present moment is all we truly have. Full engagement in the present moment contributes to a brighter future for us and those around us.

APPLICATION

Applying the knowledge, one has acquired is a crucial part of personal and professional growth. Understanding and gaining knowledge provides the basis but implementing it in practical ways brings about tangible results and helps progress towards one's goals. For attaining success, the action of putting the newfound knowledge into use allows individuals to develop their skills, build confidence, and step closer to success.

Here are some practicable ways to apply the Law of NOW:

1. **Practice Mindfulness:** Try mindfulness practice, like a body scan or a breathing exercise. These activities can help focus your mind on the present moment, anchoring your attention to your senses and promoting relaxation.

2. **Disconnect from Technology:** Taking a break from technology and spending time in nature or with loved ones can help you feel more grounded and present. It allows for a deeper connection with your surroundings and your emotions.

3. **Be Present in the Moment:** Engage fully in your present actions, whether it's during a conversation or while enjoying a meal. This practice helps amplify the experience of NOW, enhancing emotional understanding and regulation.

4. **Enjoy Personal Hobbies and Nature:** Allocate specific time to enjoy leisure activities that you love or explore the beauty of nature. This helps to step away from the distractions of past or future thoughts, keeping you grounded in the present.

5. **Indulge in Mindfulness Activities**: Whether it's through meditation, deep breathing, or simply focusing on your senses, practicing mindfulness helps maintain a strong connection with the present moment and fosters emotional wellbeing.

By consistently practicing these actions in your daily life, the Law of NOW becomes an intrinsic part of your emotional experience, enabling you to thrive in the present and build a foundation for emotional wellbeing and sound relationships.

"Happiness is not a station you arrive at, but a manner of traveling." – Margaret Lee Runbeck

THE LAW OF HAPPINESS

"May the God of hope fill you with all joy and peace as you trust in him, so that you may overflow with hope by the power of the Holy Spirit." - Romans 15:13 (NIV)

I N THE VAST OCEAN OF our emotions, happiness shines like a lighthouse, guiding us through the fog of our daily struggles, reminding us of the beauty and wonder that life holds. It's an emotion that transcends mere existence, touching every heart, crossing all barriers, and uniting us in its universal language. This journey of happiness invites us to dive deep into the sea of our emotions, to discover treasures of joy and peace hidden within.

What is happiness? Is it a fleeting spark in the dark, a distant dream we chase, or a gentle flame we kindle within our hearts? The Law of Happiness is not just a concept but a heartfelt invitation to unravel this beautiful mystery.

Imagine happiness as the warmth of a loved one's hug on a cold day, the smile that dances on your lips when a fond memory surfaces, or the quiet peace that envelops you as you watch a sunset alone. Happiness isn't confined to life's mountaintop moments; it also lives in the valleys, in the everyday, the mundane - a child's innocent giggle, the tranquil night sky, or the earthy scent after rain.

Often, we look for happiness in external achievements, in the material things we can accumulate. But the Law of Happiness gently urges us to look inward. True joy springs from the depths of our soul. It asks us to shift our gaze from chasing fleeting shadows to nurturing a garden of peace and joy within our hearts.

Happiness is often about the lens through which we view life. It's found in the most unexpected corners when we choose to see it with gratitude and hope. The Law of Happiness teaches us to embrace this perspective, to count our blessings, and to let go of the chains of resentment and attachment that hold us back.

Happiness is a melody best played in harmony with others. It finds its rhythm in shared experiences; in the empathy we offer and the connections we forge. This law emphasizes the beauty of relationships, the magic of giving joy to others, and seeing it return to us in waves of shared contentment and love.

The pursuit of happiness is a dance that lasts a lifetime, a journey of continuous discovery and growth. This chapter is a dance lesson in the art of happiness. Happiness is a step into the world of mindfulness, let our feet tap to the rhythm of gratitude, and learn to gracefully let go of what holds us back.

A STORY FROM GRACE'S KITCHEN: THE LAW OF HAPPINESS

In the heart of her home, Grace stood in her kitchen, the early morning sun casting a warm glow through the windows. Today, she was preparing her special recipe for lemon pound cake, a family favorite that brought back a myriad of joyful memories. As she zested the lemons and mixed the batter, her mind wandered to the essence of happiness.

Grace thought about how happiness, much like her baking, required a mix of different elements. It wasn't just about the sweet moments, like the sugar in her cake, but also about the zest, the little challenges, and experiences that added flavor and depth to life.

Her niece, Emily, entered the kitchen, her face clouded with the troubles of teenage life. Seeing an opportunity for a heart-to-heart conversation, Grace invited her to join in the baking. As they worked side by side, Grace listened to Emily's worries about school, friends, and the future. Each worry was like an ingredient that Emily was unsure how to mix into her life.

Grace shared her wisdom, "Happiness, my dear, is not just found in the absence of trouble. Like this cake, it's a combination of all sorts of moments - sweet, tangy, and everything in between. It's about embracing each experience and finding joy and learning in it."

As they poured the batter into the pan, Grace continued, "You see, every experience, every challenge, is an opportunity to grow, to add to your own recipe of life. And sometimes, it's the unexpected ingredients that make the most delightful flavors."

Emily listened, her frown gradually giving way to thoughtful reflection. They placed the cake in the oven, and as the aroma began to fill the kitchen, Emily smiled. It was a small but significant moment of understanding and happiness.

As they sat later, savoring the warm cake, Grace imparted one more piece of wisdom, "Remember, happiness is not just in the cake we bake, but in the baking itself, in the mixing and stirring of life, in learning, and in growing from each little moment we are given."

In the comfort of her kitchen, Grace had not only shared her recipe for lemon pound cake but also her recipe for happiness. It was a recipe that Emily would carry with her, a blend of self-awareness, acceptance, and the joy found in life's every ingredient.

CHAPTER SUMMARY

In this chapter, we embark on an emotional journey to understand and embrace the Law of Happiness. The chapter begins with a poignant reference to Romans 15:13, setting a spiritual and hopeful tone for the exploration of happiness.

The narrative delves into the essence of happiness, portraying it not just as an emotion but as a guiding light in our lives. It emphasizes that happiness transcends cultural and linguistic barriers, uniting us in a universal quest for joy and contentment.

The chapter challenges the traditional perception of happiness as a fleeting moment or a distant goal. Instead, it presents happiness as an intimate part of our everyday lives - found in simple joys, like a shared meal, time with loved ones, or a quiet moment of solitude. It encourages readers to find happiness in both extraordinary and mundane moments, suggesting that true joy lies in appreciating the beauty of everyday experiences.

A significant focus of the chapter is on the internal source of happiness. It urges a shift from seeking external validation or material success to cultivating inner peace and contentment. The chapter suggests that enduring happiness comes from within and is influenced by our perspective and attitude towards life.

The power of perspective is highlighted, showing how happiness can be discovered in unexpected places when viewed through the lens of gratitude and positivity. The chapter encourages readers to practice gratitude, acknowledge blessings, and release unnecessary attachments.

Emphasizing the communal aspect of happiness, the chapter underscores the importance of relationships, empathy, and social connection in our pursuit of joy. It illustrates how shared happiness is amplified and how giving joy to others enhances our own sense of well-being.

Finally, the chapter frames the pursuit of happiness as a lifelong journey, not a one-time achievement. It offers practical strategies and principles for cultivating lasting happiness, including mindfulness, gratitude practices, the art of letting go, and insights from positive psychology.

This chapter serves as both a guide and an inspiration, encouraging readers to weave happiness into the fabric of their daily lives. It combines theoretical insights with practical advice, resonating with themes of emotional intelligence and personal growth. The Law of Happiness is presented as an attainable, enriching path that enhances our overall quality of life and emotional well-being.

APPLICATION

Embracing and applying the Law of Happiness is essential for personal growth and emotional well-being. Knowledge of this law isn't just theoretical; its real-world application is vital for experiencing genuine joy and fulfillment in life. By actively integrating the principles of happiness, we can enhance our skills, boost our confidence, and move closer to realizing our goals of a joyful and contented life.

To effectively apply the Law of Happiness in everyday life:

1. **Cultivate Gratitude:** Begin each day by acknowledging things you are grateful for. This simple practice can shift your focus from what's missing to the abundance that already exists in your life, fostering a sense of contentment and joy.

2. **Find Joy in the Ordinary:** Make a conscious effort to find happiness in everyday moments, whether it's in a conversation, a walk in nature, or a quiet moment alone. Recognizing beauty in the ordinary can amplify your sense of happiness.

3. **Nurture Relationships:** Invest time and energy in building and maintaining meaningful relationships. The happiness we share with others not only enhances our own joy but also strengthens our connections and sense of belonging.

4. **Practice Mindfulness:** Engage in mindfulness practices such as meditation or mindful walking. Being present in the moment can help you appreciate life as it unfolds, reducing worries about the past or future.

5. **Embrace Positivity:** Foster a positive outlook on life. Challenge negative thoughts and replace them with positive affirmations. A positive mindset can significantly influence your overall happiness and perspective on life.

By integrating these actionable steps into your daily routine, you can actively embody the Law of Happiness. Doing so not only elevates your own well-being but also creates ripples of joy and positivity in your surrounding environment, contributing to a happier and more emotionally balanced life.

"The quality of our relationships determines the quality of our lives." - Esther Perel

RELATIONSHIPS & CONNECTION

"Therefore encourage one another and build each other up, just as in fact you are doing." - Thessalonians 5:11 (NIV)

"Life is like riding a bicycle, to keep your balance, you must keep moving." - Albert Einstein

THE LAW OF MOMENTUM

"Let us not become weary in doing good, for at the proper time we will reap a harvest if we do not give up."
- Galatians 6:9 (NIV)

THE PRINCIPLE OF EMOTIONAL PROPULSION or The Law of Momentum recognizes that emotional experiences can cascade, amassing momentum and shaping subsequent experiences. This law underlines the profound impact our emotional experiences can imprint on our overall emotional wellbeing.

Positive emotional encounters can thrust a wave of positivity, while conversely, negative experiences can trigger a downward emotional spiral. For instance, confronting negative emotions like sadness or anxiety can set off a domino effect of negative feelings, building momentum, and subsequently influencing future emotional experiences.

Breaking the cycle of negative momentum and nurturing positive emotional experiences necessitates us to consciously strive towards stirring positive emotions. This could involve engaging in activities that induce positive emotions, such as spending quality time with loved ones, pursuing hobbies, or participating in physical exercise.

Equally crucial is the recognition and healthy processing of negative emotional experiences. This ensures that negative emotions do not accelerate and detrimentally impact our overall emotional wellbeing.

In practical terms, this might involve seeking support from a mental health professional or a trusted peer or family member, engaging in self-care practices, or pinpointing and addressing the root causes of negative emotional experiences.

By adhering to The Law of Momentum, we can nurture a vibrant and fulfilling emotional life, and lay the groundwork for enhanced health and happiness.

A STORY FROM GRACE'S KITCHEN: THE LAW OF MOMENTUM

Every bright and early morning, Aunt Grace could be found in the heart of her home – the kitchen. The warm aroma of freshly brewed coffee filled this space, where delicious meals were not only cooked but life experiences shared and savored.

One sunny Saturday, her grandson, Robbie, was experiencing a challenge. His school project, once brimming with enthusiasm, was now bogged down by negative thoughts and frustration hounding his every effort. Sensing his despair while they were baking cookies, Aunt Grace decided to impart wisdom drawn from the Law of Momentum.

"Robbie," she began, offering up a handmade cookie, "Do you know how this cookie dough becomes a delicious treat?" A slow shake of his head encouraged her to explain further.

"It starts with a simple action. When we heat the dough in the oven, it starts a chain reaction. The baking powder we added creates gas bubbles, making the cookie rise. That's a little like our emotions, Robbie." She paused, letting the analogy sink in.

"Think of your project. You began with excitement - a positive emotion. That positive emotion could carry forth more positive feelings, helping you to work consistently and with joy, just like the rising cookie. But now, you're letting frustration set in. It's causing a negative spiral, hampering progress, akin to our cookie if we left out the baking powder." She shared empathetically, associating the real-life example to Robbie's circumstance.

"To break the negative momentum, you must reintroduce positivity. It's like adding the right ingredients to make the cookie rise. Seek help when you need it, take a small break, or focus on individual parts of your project rather than the whole," Grace advised, pointing at the now perfectly risen cookies in the oven.

That morning, within the warmth of Grace's kitchen, Robbie learned a crucial lesson about the Law of Momentum. His frustration loosened its hold, replaced by a new resolve to alter the course of his project in a more positive and effective way, kickstarting a momentum that would guide him to the completion of his project.

CHAPTER SUMMARY

The Law of Momentum details how emotional experiences can build upon one another, driving momentum, and shaping our future emotional experiences. The principal scripture for this discussion is drawn from Galatians 6:9 (NIV): "Let us not become weary in doing good, for at the proper time we will reap a harvest if we do not give up."

This law recognizes the significant role of both positive and negative emotional experiences in setting the momentum for respective outlooks. Positive experiences can enhance a positive outlook and create a positive cycle, while negative experiences can lead to a downward emotional spiral.

The chapter mentions the importance of being proactive about encouraging positive emotions to disrupt the negative momentum. This could encompass engaging in activities that trigger positive emotions, such as spending quality time with loved ones, pursuing hobbies, or engaging in physical exercise.

Moreover, acknowledging and constructively processing negative emotional experiences is crucial for halting negative momentum and preventing negative impact on overall emotional wellbeing. Practical steps to accomplish this may include seeking professional mental support, undertaking self-care practices, or identifying and addressing the root causes of negative emotional experiences.

By honoring the Law of Momentum, we can foster a positive and fulfilling emotional life and lay a strong foundation for greater health and happiness.

APPLICATION

Applying the knowledge, one has gathered is an integral part of both personal and professional growth. It is insufficient to simply acquire knowledge – it must be executed in practical ways to yield actual results and progress towards one's objectives. By utilizing newfound knowledge, individuals can cultivate their abilities, bolster confidence, and inch closer to success.

To apply the Law of Momentum:

1. **Celebrate Accomplishments:** Record the three things you've accomplished in the past week and celebrate them. Recognizing and rejoicing in your progress helps maintain positive momentum.

2. **Manageable Tasks:** Construct a list of small, manageable tasks that lead towards a bigger goal. Progress, no matter how small, gives momentum to your efforts.

3. **Setting Goals:** Establish a new goal and formulate a plan to accomplish it. Having clear targets and a plan of action fuels the momentum needed for achievement.

4. **Celebrate Progress:** No matter how minor, celebrate your progress along the way. This positive reinforcement aids in sustaining the momentum.

5. **Visualize Success:** Envision your success and have faith in your capacity to achieve your objectives. Visualization is a powerful tool to generate and maintain momentum towards your goals.

Remember, the principle of the Law of Momentum is not about grand, sweeping changes but rather the consistent, small steps that snowball into big shifts in our lives over time.

"Nobody can hurt me without my permission." - Mahatma Gandhi

THE LAW OF DIMINISHMENT

"Do not be anxious about anything, but in every situation, by prayer and petition, with thanksgiving, present your requests to God. And the peace of God, which transcends all understanding, will guard your hearts and your minds in Christ Jesus." - Philippians 4:6-7 (NIV)

THE LAW OF DIMINISHMENT POSITS that emotional experiences can fade over time, especially when they remain unacknowledged or unexpressed. It's crucial to identify and process emotional experiences to prevent them from diminishing and negatively impacting wellbeing.

This law signifies the necessity of healthily and constructively recognizing and processing emotional events to impede their gradual reduction and subsequent adverse effects on our emotional wellbeing.

Ignoring to process and recognize emotional experiences can lead to their suppression, inflicting a detrimental effect on our overall emotional wellbeing. Such neglect can surface a host of negative after-effects, among them amplified stress, anxiety, and difficulties in regulating emotions.

Preventing the adverse consequences of emotional diminishment calls for healthy, constructive acknowledgement and processing of emotional experiences. This could involve practices like journaling, talk therapy, or creative expression, bolstered by support from mental health professionals, trusted friends, or family members.

In addition, there is great importance to nurture emotional cognizance and identify instances when emotional experiences are suppressed or minimized. This proactive approach empowers us to address emotional experiences before their impact becomes negative on our emotional wellbeing.

In practical terms, this could entail undertaking regular emotional check-ins and allocating time on a routine basis to process emotional experiences. Seeking support from mental health professionals or loved ones, especially when emotional experiences seem overwhelming or complex to process, could also be part of this practice.

By respecting the Law of Diminishment, we can prevent emotional experiences from inducing a detrimental effect on our emotional wellbeing, consequently fostering a harmonious and fulfilling emotional life.

A STORY FROM GRACE'S FAMILY ROOM: THE LAW OF DIMINISHMENT

Aunt Grace was often nestled in her cozy family room when discussing the intricacies of relationships. On one such evening, with a heartwarming fire crackling in the fireplace and the room filled with family and a few close friends, the topic of conversation shifted to emotional experiences.

One of her friends, Marianne, was confiding about a fading emotional connection with her sister. Their once close relationship had been deteriorating over time, and Marianne was distraught, feeling a sense of loss.

Listening empathetically, Grace recognized this as a perfect moment to share the wisdom of the Law of Diminishment.

"Marianne," Grace began gently, "our emotional experiences are a lot like this fire." She gestured towards the hearth before them. "If we don't stoke them, give them attention, they start to diminish."

"The Law of Diminishment teaches us those emotions, when not acknowledged or expressed, can fade over time, much like your connection with your sister. It's crucial to recognize and process these emotions to prevent them from disappearing completely and impacting your wellbeing negatively."

As she spoke, Grace added a new log into the fire, stoking it gently. "To reignite the emotional connection, you might need to confront and express your feelings respectfully to your sister."

"Remember, emotional experiences like the fire before us, if attended to, can warm us, but if neglected, they dwindle and turn cold," Grace ended with a comforting smile.

That evening, in the embrace of the family room, Aunt Grace, with her compassionate wisdom, enlightened her friends and family about the Law of Diminishment. As the fire crackled cheerfully once more, Marianne found a new resolve, ready to rebuild the emotional bridge with her sister.

CHAPTER SUMMARY

The Law of Diminishment revolves around the concept that unacknowledged or unexpressed emotional experiences can fade over time. Building upon a scripture from Philippians 4:6-7 (NIV), "Do not be anxious about anything, but in every situation, by prayer and petition, with thanksgiving, present your requests to God. And the peace of God, which transcends all understanding, will guard your hearts and your minds in Christ Jesus," the chapter exemplifies how vital it is to recognize and process emotional experiences to prevent their diminishment and potential negative impact on wellbeing.

The Law of Diminishment highlights the significance of recognizing and processing emotional experiences healthily and constructively, to block them from fading and ruining our emotional wellbeing. It underscores the importance of understanding the impact that our emotional experiences can have on our overall emotional state.

The chapter draws attention to the consequences of neglecting to process emotional experiences— these can be repressed and negatively affect our emotional wellbeing. This can lead to various negative outcomes, including increased stress, anxiety, and difficulty managing emotions.

To prevent these negative consequences, it's crucial to acknowledge and process emotional experiences in a healthy, constructive manner. This could involve journaling, talk therapy, or creative expression, as well as seeking support from mental health professionals or trusted friends and family members.

The chapter reinforces the importance of emotional awareness and identification of repressed or diminished emotional experiences. By doing so, proactive steps can be taken to address these emotional experiences before they impact our emotional wellbeing negatively.

By honoring the Law of Diminishment, we can not only prevent emotional experiences from detrimentally affecting our emotional wellbeing but also cultivate a more positive and fulfilling emotional life.

APPLICATION

The act of applying acquired knowledge is a crucial contributor to personal and professional growth. Merely gaining knowledge is not sufficient; it must be practically implemented to witness tangible results and progress towards one's objectives. By doing so, individuals can enhance their skills, foster confidence, and take strides towards success.

To practically enforce the Law of Diminishment:

1. **Thought Replacement:** Write down a recurring negative thought, then consciously replace it with a positive affirmation. This practice instigates the process of reversing potential emotional diminishment.

2. **Self-compassion and Self-care:** Consciously practice self-compassion and indulge in self-care, especially during periods of emotional lows. This aids in acknowledging and addressing negative emotional experiences.

3. **Kindness to Oneself:** During challenging times, being generous and kind to oneself is key. This step assists in clearing barriers set up by ongoing negative feelings.

4. **Happiness List:** Create a list of things that bring joy and refer to it when in need of a positive boost. This can serve as a counter to the potential for emotional experiences to diminish over time.

5. **Positive Self-talk:** Regularly practice positive self-talk and switch out negative thoughts with affirming statements. This

effort can fortify the process of preventing negative emotions from fading away and negatively impacting overall wellbeing.

By employing these measures, we can actively reduce the likelihood of emotional diminishment, thereby nurturing emotional wellbeing and cultivating a positive emotional life.

"We are not separate from one another, and when one suffers, we all suffer." - Krista Tippett

THE LAW OF CONTAGION

"A cheerful heart is good medicine, but a crushed spirit dries up the bones." - Proverbs 17:22 (NIV)

EMOTIONS POSSESS THE ABILITY TO become contagious, transmitting from one individual to another. The Law of Contagion puts focus on how our emotional states can influence those around us and guides towards the cultivation of positive emotional experiences that can be shared with others.

When we undergo positive emotions, such as joy, enthusiasm, or love, these emotions can permeate to those in our vicinity, aiding in fostering positive emotional experiences and enhancing social connections. Conversely, negative emotions like sadness or nervousness can also ripple out to those around us, engendering a negative emotional ambiance and weakening social ties.

The key to promoting positive emotional contagion lies in fostering positive emotional encounters and sharing these experiences intentionally with others. Such practices can incorporate engaging in activities that boost positive emotions, like spending quality time with loved ones, exploring hobbies, or partaking in physical exercise.

It is equally crucial to remain aware of the impact our emotions can have on others and consciously cultivate positive emotional contagion in interactions. This can often involve being present and engaged in social interactions, expressing empathy, and understanding others' emotional experiences, and sharing positive emotional experiences intentionally with those around us.

Practically, this could involve regular emotional check-ins with loved ones, intentional creation of a positive emotional atmosphere at home or workplace and seeking opportunities to share positive emotional experiences with those around us.

By adhering to the Law of Contagion, we contribute to an environment of emotional support and understanding, promoting positive emotional experiences not only for ourselves but also for those around us.

A Story from Grace's Porch: The Law of Contagion

Settled on her welcoming porch, Aunt Grace often found herself surrounded by loved ones, discussing topics of social awareness and empathy. The porch, overlooking her beautifully manicured garden, was a place of quiet contemplation and shared wisdom.

One balmy evening, a small group had gathered. Laughter and light-hearted banter floated across the porch, accompanied by the occasional clink of iced tea glasses. Grace's friend, Lisa, was sharing her difficulties at work, particularly with a co-worker who constantly radiated negativity.

Sensing Lisa's distressed state, Grace saw an opportunity to share her wisdom on the Law of Contagion.

"Lisa, dear," Grace started, leaning back in her rocking chair, "Emotions are powerful enough to spread amongst us - much like a virus."

Her friends seemed taken aback, their eyes reflecting a mix of intrigue and surprise.

"It's called the Law of Contagion," she went on. "Just as laughter can be infectious, spreading joy, so too can negative emotions spread, creating an uneasy atmosphere. Your co-worker's negativity is affecting you and possibly others around."

Grace paused to sip her iced tea, then continued, "But we can counter this. We can influence with positivity, love, and kindness. When we consciously radiate these, it encourages a positive atmosphere. Even the most negative people can't resist an infectious smile!"

She concluded with a jovial wink. Laughter bubbled up on the porch as all eyes turned to Lisa, her previous distress replaced with a contemplative smile.

That evening, under the tranquil porch lighting, Aunt Grace demonstrated the profound nature of the Law of Contagion. As the gathering dispersed later, they left with a renewed sense of resolution to spread more positivity in their own social circles, aware that their emotional "temperature" could indeed affect their surroundings.

CHAPTER SUMMARY

The Law of Contagion asserts that emotions can be infectious, capable of transmitting from one person to another. A guiding verse from Proverbs 17:22 (NIV) states "A cheerful heart is good medicine, but a crushed spirit dries up the bones."

The Law of Contagion acknowledges the profound impact our emotions can have on those around us and offers guidance on cultivating positive emotional experiences and sharing them with others.

Positive emotions, such as joy, excitement, love, can ripple out to those around us, elevating the overall emotional atmosphere and strengthening social connections. In contrast, negative emotions such as sadness or anxiety can permeate a social environment, leading to a negative emotional atmosphere and possibly weakening relationships.

To encourage the contagion of positive emotions, this law advises nurturing positive emotional experiences and intentionally sharing these with others. This can involve engaging in activities that generate positive emotions, such as spending quality time with loved ones, pursuing hobbies, or engaging in physical exercise.

Moreover, it's vital to be aware of our emotions' impact on others and consciously cultivate a positive emotional contagion during interactions with others. This involves being fully present and engaged during social interactions, expressing empathy for others' emotional experiences, and intentionally communicating positive emotional experiences with those around us.

Practically, this could involve performing regular emotional check-ins with loved ones, consciously establishing a positive emotional atmosphere in our living, or working spaces and seeking occasions to share positive experiences with others.

By adhering to the Law of Contagion, we can contribute to an emotionally supportive and understanding environment and promote positive emotional experiences for ourselves and extend these experiences to those around us.

APPLICATION

Applying obtained knowledge is a critical part of personal and professional growth. It is inadequate to just acquire knowledge - it is necessary to apply it to realize concrete results and advance towards one's goals. By employing newfound knowledge, individuals can enhance their skills, elevate their confidence, and progressively approach success.

To act upon the Law of Contagion:

1. **Share Compliments:** Give a genuine compliment to someone and observe the resulting feel-good emotion for both parties. This simple act can spark a ripple of positivity.

2. **Practice Kindness:** Cultivate a habit of being kind to yourself and others, even in small ways. Kindness can act as a contagious catalyst for positive emotions.

3. **Smile at Strangers:** Offer a smile to strangers on your path. Such small gestures of goodwill can spread positivity and light up someone else's day.

4. **Gratitude Practice:** Dedicate time each day to consciously reflect on the positive things in your life. regular practice of gratitude can foster a positive mindset and serve as an emotional contagion.

5. **Surround Yourself with Positivity:** Spend time with people who inspire and uplift you. Their positive outlook can influence your emotional state for the better.

Implementing these methods not only ensures you're contributing positively to the emotional atmosphere around you, but also reinforces your own emotional wellbeing, according to the Law of Contagion.

"The quality of our relationships determines the quality of our lives." - Esther Perel

THE LAW OF RELATIONSHIPS

"Therefore encourage one another and build each other up, just as in fact you are doing." - 1 Thessalonians 5:11 (NIV)

OUR EMOTIONAL EXPERIENCES ARE OFTEN deeply woven within the fabric of relationships. Endowed with the power to promote emotional wellbeing and assist in the processing of emotional encounters, relationships play a critical role. This Law of Relationships underscores the importance of emotional connectivity and social support in fostering emotional wellbeing and nurturing positive emotional experiences.

Positive relationships, whether it be with friends, family, or the community, often provide a sense of belonging, emotional support, and understanding. Cultivating such relationships could result in stimulation of positive emotions such as joy, love, and happiness.

Contrarily, negative relationships can trigger stress, anxiety, and elevate negative emotions. It then becomes crucial to consciously nurture positive relationships and establish healthy boundaries with those who potentially negatively affect our emotional wellbeing.

Promotion of positive relationships can be achieved by intentional construction and maintenance of social connections. This could include activities promoting social bonding, including joining community groups or clubs, participating in social events, or spending quality time with loved ones.

Expressing empathy, understanding, and support towards those around us is also vital. Showing care and assurance of being there for someone can enhance social connections, propagating positive emotional experiences for self and others.

In practicality, it could involve active participation in social events, earmarking time each day to interact with dear ones, and intentional expression of empathy and support during these interactions.

Dedicatedly adhering to the Law of Relationships enables cultivation of positive emotional experiences and a culture of emotional understanding and support. Acknowledging the deep connection our relationships have with our emotional wellbeing and by fostering positive relationships can build a robust and more positive emotional life.

A STORY FROM GRACE'S FAMILY ROOM: THE LAW OF RELATIONSHIPS

Nestled in her warm and welcoming family room, Aunt Grace reveled in conversations about relationships. The family room, with its soft lighting and comfortable furnishings, was a place of open dialogue and shared wisdom. One such evening, the conversation turned to the shifting dynamics in the lives of her family and friends.

Her niece, Lucy, was struggling in navigating her relationship with her college roommate. Their bond, initially close, was under strain with stress from the final exams approaching. Observing Lucy's distress, Grace decided to share insights about the Law of Relationships.

"Lucy," Grace began, her voice calm and comforting, "Our relationships, like plants in a garden, need nurturing. They are interconnected with our emotions and can impact our wellbeing."

"The Law of Relationships reminds us of the strength in emotional connections and social support. Positive relationships offer a sense of belonging, emotional support, and understanding." She paused, offering a reassuring smile.

"However, if they become negative and strained, they can harbor stress and anxiety. It's important to nurture these relationships consciously and foster positivity." Grace advised, her eyes glinting in the cozy room's soft light.

"In your case, instead of allowing the stress to strain your relationship with your roommate, why not turn this into an opportunity to support one another during the exam period? You can study together, help each other maintain a positive environment. Remember, empathy, understanding, and support are pillars in relationships." Grace concluded.

In the warmth of the family room, Grace had unpacked the Law of Relationships. Lucy, absorbing her aunt's wisdom, felt a renewed strength to mend her strained relationship. That room, filled with family and friends, was a witness to Grace's wisdom, imparting to each of them an understanding of the profound connection between emotional well-being and relationships.

CHAPTER SUMMARY

The Law of Relationships encapsulates the intertwined nature of emotions and relationships. Citing a verse from 1 Thessalonians 5:11 (NIV), "Therefore encourage one another and build each other up, just as in fact you are doing," the chapter underscores the influence relationships hold over emotional wellbeing.

This law emphasizes the powerful role of social support and emotional connection in fostering emotional wellbeing and nurturing positive emotional experiences. Positive relationships with friends, family, and the community can instill a sense of belonging, offering emotional support and understanding. It acknowledges that when positive relationships are nurtured, we're more likely to experience positive emotions, such as happiness, love, and joy.

However, the chapter also highlights that negative relationships can lead to distress, heightening stress, anxiety, and negative emotions. It establishes the importance of being strategic about cultivating positive relationships and setting healthy boundaries with those who might have a negative influence on our emotional wellbeing.

To encourage positive relationships, it's important to be attentive towards building and maintaining social connections. Participating in social activities, joining groups or clubs, or spending quality time with loved ones are suggested paths to venture. It also underlines the significance of expressing empathy, understanding, and support for those around us which can bolster social connections and foster positive experiences collectively.

In practical terms, proactive participation in social rituals, dedicating time each day to interact with loved ones, and intentional expression of empathy and support during such interactions are recommended.

By abiding by the Law of Relationships, a culture of emotional understanding, support, and positive emotional experiences can be cultivated. Recognizing the deep nexus between relationships and emotional well-being, the cultivation of positive relationships is deemed essential for constructing a more robust, positive emotional life.

APPLICATION

Acquired knowledge's application is a significant component of personal and professional growth. It's counterproductive to merely accumulate knowledge - it must be pragmatically implemented to manifest tangible results and make progress toward your objectives. Concept application enables individuals to refine their abilities, boost confidence, and progressively achieve success.

Here are some practical ways to implement the Law of Relationships:

1. **Express Appreciation:** Draft a letter or send a message to someone you appreciate. Expressing appreciation not only strengthens your relationships but also fosters shared positive emotions.

2. **Active Listening and Empathy:** During your conversations, practice active listening and show empathy. This helps in deepening your understanding of others' experiences and emotions, thereby strengthening your relationships.

3. **Quality Time:** Plan and prioritize fun activities with your friends or loved ones. Quality time together can fortify relationships and create a supportive environment for sharing and managing emotions.

4. **Understand Others' Perspectives:** Strive to understand the perspectives of others. This practice promotes empathy, an essential pillar for building strong, positive relationships.

5. **Show Gratitude:** Show genuine appreciation for people in your life and express gratitude for their presence. Acknowledging the support and love they provide can nurture your relationships, promoting emotional wellbeing.

By practicing these measures, you can enhance your understanding and application of the Law of Relationships, fostering positive relationships that support emotional wellbeing for yourself and others.

"It is not the strongest of the species that survives, nor the most intelligent; it is the one most adaptable to change." - Charles Darwin

THE PATH OF ADAPTABILITY & CHANGE

"Therefore, we do not lose heart. Though outwardly we are wasting away, yet inwardly we are being renewed day by day." - 2 Corinthians 4:16 (NIV)

"Attention is the rarest and purest form of generosity." - Simone Weil

THE LAW OF INATTENTION

"So then, each of us will give an account of ourselves to God." - Romans 14:12 (NIV)

NEGLECT OR INATTENTION TOWARDS EMOTIONS can lead to unfavorable consequences which are seen as increased stress, difficulty in emotion regulation, and decreased emotional wellbeing. The Law of Inattention brings focus to the importance of mindfulness and intentionality in respect to our emotional experiences while providing guidance to cultivate positive emotional experiences and to prevent negative emotions from building.

The intensity of negative emotions such as anxiety, fear, and sadness can expand when ignored or suppressed, leading to increased stress, compromised emotional wellbeing, and difficulty in emotion regulation.

Alternatively, positive emotions like joy, love, and gratitude can dim and disappear if not attended to and nurtured appropriately. By not cultivating positive emotions, we risk losing opportunities for emotional growth and enrichment.

To honor the Law of Inattention, it is crucial to practice mindfulness and intentionality in our emotional experiences. These practices can include reserving time each day to understand, identify, and process negative emotions in a healthful and constructive manner.

It's also fundamental to actively cultivate positive emotions such as joy, love, and gratitude and take relevant steps to nurture them by participating in activities that foster positive emotions like spending quality time with loved ones, indulging in hobbies, or partaking in physical exercise.

It's crucial to remember that the reaction to our emotions is a matter of choice. Although the circumstances triggering these emotions may be beyond control, the response to them is within control. By choosing to adopt mindfulness and intentionality in our emotional experiences, we can inhibit negative emotions from augmenting and cultivate positive emotional experiences leading to emotional wellbeing and fulfillment.

In practice, this could involve incorporating regular self-care practices such as mindfulness or meditation and taking time out each day to reflect upon our emotional experiences. It may also involve seeking help from mental health professionals or trusted ones when dealing with overwhelming or hard-to-navigate negative emotions.

By revering the Law of Inattention, we can prevent the surge of negative emotions and cultivate a positive, fulfilling emotional life. Remember, we always have the choice to be intentional and mindful about our emotional experiences, allowing us to pursue greater emotional well-being and fulfillment.

A STORY FROM GRACE'S KITCHEN: THE LAW OF INATTENTION

The kitchen for Aunt Grace was always bustling - a comforting medley of aromas and a hotspot of wisdom, particularly when it came to dialogues about self-awareness. Surrounded by glittering pots and the comforting hum of the oven, Grace often shared her observations on life.

One afternoon, her nephew Ryan had joined her in the kitchen, revealing his troubles with overwhelming frustration he was pushing aside to 'deal with it later.' Seeing his struggle, Grace recognized the opportunity to impart the wisdom of the Law of Inattention.

"Ryan, dear," Grace started, as she gently stirred a pot of simmering soup, "emotions are a lot like this soup here. If we forget about it and let it simmer too long without giving it the attention it needs, it could easily boil-over, creating a mess."

"Inattention to our emotions - negative or positive, can have effects we might not foresee. When neglected, negative feelings like your frustration can intensify, leading to increased stress and decreased emotional wellbeing."

Grace paused to taste the soup, adjusting the seasoning, "On the other hand, positive emotions too need care. Joy, love, gratitude—they need attention just like our flavorful soup here. If not tended to, positive feelings and experiences might lose their potency, fading away."

"So, Ryan, it's necessary to be mindful with emotions, much like we're attentive to our soup cooking. Check-in with yourself, try to understand and process your feelings in a healthy way, and remember to cultivate and savor the positive moments." Grace concluded warmly.

That afternoon, inside the warm, aroma-filled kitchen, Grace unfolded the profound Law of Inattention. Ryan listened, absorbing the wisdom that came interspersed with his aunt's soup stirring. As he left the kitchen later, his steps were lighter, armed with a newfound understanding of managing his feelings, realizing the importance of providing due attention to his emotions.

CHAPTER SUMMARY

The Law of Inattention brings attention to the potential negative repercussions of disregarding our emotions. Backed by the verse from Romans 14:12 (NIV) - "So then, each of us will give an account of ourselves to God," the chapter stresses the importance of self-accountability with our emotional care.

A lack of attention towards our emotions can lead to increased stress, difficulty regulating emotions, and decreased emotional wellbeing. The law indicates the significance of being mindful and intentional about our emotional experiences, offering guidance to cultivate positive emotional experiences and prevent negative emotions from escalating.

Negative emotions such as anxiety, fear, and sadness can grow in intensity when ignored or suppressed. Conversely, positive emotions such as joy, love, and gratitude can fade away when they aren't attended to and nurtured. The failure to nurture positive emotions may result in missed opportunities for emotional growth and satisfaction.

To honor the Law of Inattention, mindfulness, and intentional attention towards our emotional experiences are crucial. It might involve dedicating time each day to understand, identify, and process negative emotions in a healthful and constructive manner. It's also important to intentionally cultivate and nurture positive emotions through activities such as spending quality time with loved ones, indulging in hobbies, or engaging in physical exercise.

Our response to emotional triggers is ultimately a matter of choice. By choosing to be mindful and intentional about our emotional experiences, we can counteract the amplification of negative emotions and cultivate positive emotional experiences, leading to emotional well-being and fulfillment.

In practice, regular self-care practices such as mindfulness or meditation, daily reflection on emotional experiences, and seeking support when negative emotions are overwhelming or hard to handle can be helpful.

By respecting the Law of Inattention, we can prevent the proliferation of negative emotions and build a positive and fulfilling emotional life. Emotions should be treated with consciousness and mindfulness, promoting greater emotional wellbeing and fulfillment.

APPLICATION

Transforming acquired knowledge into action is a pivotal aspect of personal and professional growth. It's not sufficient to merely amass knowledge; this knowledge needs to be actively applied to yield tangible results and further progress towards individual goals. Implementation of newfound knowledge allows individuals to evolve their skills, build self-confidence, and consistently move towards success.

To implement the Law of Inattention:

1. **Single tasking**: Dedicate your attention to one task at a time. In a world hooked on multi-tasking, single-tasking bolsters focus and mindfulness towards your current activity.

2. **Live in the Moment**: Temporarily set aside multitasking and make an active effort to be fully present in the moment. This

helps in attentive observation and processing of surrounding experiences, including emotions.

3. **Mindfulness Practice:** Apply mindfulness by concentrating on one task at a time. Endeavor to be fully absorbed in the moment, which helps foster both attention to emotions and productivity.

4. **Prioritize Important Tasks:** Halt multitasking for a while and prioritize your most crucial task first. By focusing your attention on important tasks, you can manage your emotional state more effectively.

5. **Relaxation Techniques:** Incorporate relaxation techniques such as deep breathing exercises or progressive muscle relaxation to manage stress levels and enhance focus. These techniques often provide a space to check in with your emotional state, promoting overall emotional well-being.

By adopting these methods, we can better attend to our emotional health, ensuring that neither positive nor negative experiences are neglected, as per the Law of Inattention.

"The greatest weapon against stress is our ability to choose one thought over another." - William James

THE LAW OF FOCUS

"Let your eyes look straight ahead; fix your gaze directly before you." - Proverbs 4:25 (NIV)

FOLLOWING THE WORDS IN PROVERBS 4:25, the principle of emotional concentration or the Law of Focus sheds light on the significant role focus and attention play in emotional processing and regulation.

Our emotional experiences mold under the influence of our focus and attention. This law underscores the importance of intentionality in directing our attention, providing guidance for fostering positive emotional experiences, and curbing the growth of negative emotions.

When attention is centered on negative experiences or emotions, such as anxiety, fear, or sadness, the likelihood of experiencing such emotions intensifies. Conversely, focusing on positive experiences or emotions, such as joy, love, and gratitude, enhances the probability of experiencing these positive emotions.

To foster positive emotional experiences, intentionality in directing our attention becomes crucial. This could encompass practices like mindfulness or meditation, as well as carving out opportunities to focus on positive experiences and emotions.

Awareness of the impact that thoughts and beliefs can exert on emotional experiences is also significant. By nurturing positive thoughts and beliefs, we can shift our focus to positive emotional experiences, preventing negative emotions from amplifying.

In practical terms, this could involve engaging in regular self-reflection and identifying any negative thought patterns or beliefs that may contribute to negative emotional experiences. It could also involve seeking support from mental health professionals or trusted ones when encountering overwhelming or difficult-to-handle negative emotions.

By adhering to the Law of Focus, a positive and fulfilling emotional life can be fostered. Remember, the shaping of our emotional experiences is influenced by the focus of our attention. By intentionally directing our attention, we can nurture positive emotional experiences and prevent the amplification of negative emotions.

A STORY FROM GRACE'S GARDEN: THE LAW OF FOCUS

Aunt Grace's garden was a vibrant canvas of blossoming flowers and bustling greenery, serving as the perfect backdrop for discussions around self-management. Grace was a firm believer that a garden served as an analogy for life's lessons, especially for understanding the Law of Focus.

Her neighbor, Sarah, was often overwhelmed. She split her attention between numerous tasks and worries, causing her stress levels to rise and her struggle with negative emotions.

Strolling through her garden, pruning, and tending to her plants, Grace addressed Sarah's concerns with the analogy of a gardener's focus.

"Sarah, dear," she began, holding a rose fascicle gently, "Just look at these roses. To help them bloom beautifully, I direct my focus towards their needs: the right amount of water, and sunlight, and pruning the unnecessary parts. Now, apply this 'gardener's focus' to your emotions."

"The Law of Focus suggests that our emotional experiences are largely shaped by where we direct our attention. If we consistently focus on negative experiences or emotions, they'll grow, just as weeds do when left unchecked. But if we consciously focus our 'watering and sunlight' – our energy and attention – on positive emotions, we'll be fostering our 'roses' of joy, love, and gratitude." Grace explained.

"Take time for practices like mindfulness, meditation, focusing on positive experiences. Remember to prune away the negative thought patterns or beliefs that might be contributing to your emotional distress. You can always reach out to professionals or loved ones when things feel overwhelming." Grace concluded her analogy.

Beneath the canopy of fresh leaves and colorful blooms, Grace had masterfully unboxed the Law of Focus to Sarah. As they finished their gardening routine and went back inside, Sarah felt a renewed sense of control over her emotional garden, ready to become a mindful gardener of her emotions.

CHAPTER SUMMARY

The Law of Focus emphasizes the significance of focus and attention for emotional processing and regulation. Linked to a verse from Proverbs 4:25 (NIV), "Let your eyes look straight ahead; fix your gaze directly before you," this chapter accentuates the need for attentiveness in emotional health.

Our emotional experiences are powerfully shaped by the focus of our attention. The Law of Focus underscores the important role of being intentional about where we direct our attention, providing guidance for the cultivation of positive emotional experiences and the prevention of escalating negative emotions.

When our focus is centered on negative experiences or emotions, we're more likely to experience negative emotions such as anxiety, fear, and sadness. Conversely, when we focus on positive experiences or emotions, we're more likely to experience positive emotions, such as joy, love, and gratitude.

Promoting positive emotional experiences involves intentionality in directing our attention. This could involve engaging in mindfulness or meditation practices and seeking out opportunities to concentrate on positive experiences and emotions.

Being aware of the impact of our thoughts and beliefs on our emotional experiences is also critical. By cultivating positive thoughts and beliefs, we can shift our focus towards positive emotional experiences and prevent negative emotions from escalating.

In practice, this may involve self-reflection, identification of negative thought patterns or beliefs contributing to negative emotional experiences and seeking support from mental health professionals or trusted ones when negative emotions feel overwhelming.

The Law of Focus is honored by fostering a positive, fulfilling emotional life. Our emotional experiences are profoundly shaped by our attention focus. By being intentional about where we direct our attention, we can cultivate positive emotional experiences and prevent negative emotions from taking hold.

APPLICATION

Implementing acquired knowledge is an essential component of personal and professional development. The acquisition of knowledge isn't sufficient in itself; the implementation of knowledge in a practical manner ensures significant results and aids in progressing towards one's aspirations. Enacting newfound knowledge allows for skills development, confidence enhancement, and gradual movement towards success.

To practically implement the Law of Focus:

1. **Prioritize Tasks:** Develop and stick to a daily schedule, prioritizing your most important tasks. Organization can help in honing your focus and boosting efficiency.

2. **Present Moment Focus:** Practice being present and entirely focused on the task at hand. Maintaining focus can aid in managing emotional experiences effectively.

3. **Daily Task Planning:** Reiterate creating a daily schedule, enlisting, and prioritizing the significant tasks of the day. Regular planning can streamline your focus and attention.

4. **Minimize Distractions:** Remove potential disruptions, be it turning off your phone, clearing up your workspace, or finding a serene place to work. A distraction-free environment promotes better focus.

5. **Visualization Practices:** Indulge in visualization techniques, envisioning yourself successfully completing the ongoing task. Visualization guides focus and propels positive emotional experiences.

By following these approaches, we can better understand and apply the Law of Focus, thereby cultivating positive emotional experiences, and mitigating the rise of negative emotions.

"The future belongs to those who understand that relevance is a matter of being the right thing, in the right place, at the right time." - Seth Godin

THE LAW OF RELEVANCE

"For we are God's handiwork, created in Christ Jesus to do good works, which God prepared in advance for us to do." - Ephesians 2:10 (NIV)

T HE FOUNDATION OF THE LAW of Relevance is expressed through Ephesians 2:10 (NIV), which advocates the necessity to analyze the relevance of emotional experiences for deeper comprehension and processing.

Our emotional experiences often shape around relevance – their alignment with our self-concept and our values. The Law of Relevance acknowledges the importance of intentionality about our values and priorities to nurture positive emotional experiences and to inhibit negative emotions from escalating.

When our experiences resonate with our values and priorities, we're more likely to encounter positive emotions like joy, love, and gratitude. In contrast, incongruence between our experiences and values could lead to negative emotions like anxiety, fear, and sadness.

Promoting positive emotional experiences calls for intentional alignment with our values and priorities, seeking experiences and opportunities compatible with them. This could involve participation in activities yielding personal growth and contentment, like indulging in hobbies, engaging in volunteer work, or spending quality time with loved ones.

Awareness is also required about the influence our values and priorities can wield over our emotional experiences. Establishing realistic and optimistic values and priorities can foster a sense of purpose, prevent negative emotions from taking hold and encourage fulfillment.

In practical terms, this could mean engaging in regular self-reflection, identification of our values and priorities, and seeking opportunities harmonious with them. Seeking support from mental health professionals or confidants when negative emotions feel overwhelming or challenging to process could also be part of this practice.

By honoring the Law of Relevance, we can cultivate a fulfilling emotional life charged with positivity. It's crucial to remember, our emotional experiences are frequently shaped by the relevance they hold to our sense of self and values. By being intentional about our values and priorities, we can foster positive emotional experiences and prevent the aggravation of negative emotions.

A Story from Grace's Porch: The Law of Relevance

Aunt Grace's porch, with its welcoming rocking chairs and views of the community, was the chosen spot for conversations about social awareness and empathy. It was on this porch that Grace unwrapped the Law of Relevance to James, a friend from the neighborhood.

James was struggling to find joy in the community's annual fundraiser, which he dutifully attended each year although it wasn't of personal interest. Observing this, Grace chose to converse about the importance of aligning one's emotions with personal values and priorities.

"James," Grace began, her eyes reflecting the gentle afternoon light, "Sometimes, we partake in activities that don't truly align with our personal values or passions, and that can manifest in a swirl of negative emotions."

"Remember the Law of Relevance. Our emotional experiences often shape up based on their relevance to our sense of self and our values." Grace continued. She gestured to the community visible from the porch, "If the fundraiser doesn't align with your interests or values, it might be why you're feeling this way. Your emotion is telling you that there's a lack of relevance."

"To foster positive emotional experiences, align actions with personal values. Seek out activities that resonate with your values and priorities. Spend time on things that bring you joy, fulfillment, things that are relevant to you." Grace advised.

That afternoon on Grace's porch, amidst the comfortable rocking chairs and scenic views, the Law of Relevance took form in that shared wisdom. James walked away with a better understanding of his emotions and a decision to find activities more aligned with his values, ensuring that his emotional experiences would, from then on, have a deeper relevance to him.

CHAPTER SUMMARY

The Law of Relevance, as it is defined in the verse from Ephesians 2:10 (NIV), "For we are God's handiwork, created in Christ Jesus to do good works, which God prepared in advance for us to do," emphasizes the significance of analyzing the relevance of our emotional experiences in order to better comprehend and navigate them.

Our emotional states often take shape around the relevance of our experiences corresponding to our sense of self and our values. This law recognizes the importance of being intentional about our values and priorities for the cultivation of positive emotional experiences and the prevention of escalating negative emotions.

When our experiences align with our values and priorities, we are more likely to encounter positive emotions such as joy, love, and gratitude. However, experiences that are in dissonance with our values and priorities may result in negative emotions like anxiety, fear, and sadness.

Fostering positive emotional experiences hinges on being intentional about our values and priorities and seeking experiences and opportunities aligned with them. This could involve activities that cater to personal growth and satisfaction, such as hobbies, volunteering, or quality time with loved ones.

Understanding the impact that our values and priorities can have on our emotional experiences is also important. By establishing realistic, positive values and priorities, one can cultivate a sense of purpose and satisfaction and prevent negative emotions from taking hold.

In practice, this could involve regular self-reflection and identification of our values and priorities, and actively seeking experiences and opportunities that align with them. It could also involve seeking support from mental health professionals or loved ones when negative emotions feel overwhelming.

By honoring the Law of Relevance, we can cultivate a positive and rewarding emotional life. Remembering that our emotional states are often shaped by the relevance of our experiences to our self-concept and values, by actively directing our attention towards our values and priorities, we can foster positive emotional experiences and prevent negative emotions from taking hold.

APPLICATION

The process of applying the knowledge one acquires plays a crucial role in both personal and professional growth. Merely harvesting knowledge is insufficient; it needs to be applied pragmatically to yield tangible results and to progress toward set targets. By incorporating newfound knowledge into action, one can develop their skills, enhance self-confidence, and keep sailing towards success.

Implementing the Law of Relevance practically calls for:

1. **Presence and Awareness:** Practice being both present and aware of the needs of those around you. Active recognition of others' needs can help foster stronger, more empathetic relationships.

2. **Intention in Interaction:** Set an intention to be more present and aware in your daily interactions. This practice can help ensure your actions align with your values and can improve overall emotional experiences.

3. **Service to Others:** Set an intention to serve others. It can be through various ways: volunteering or simple acts of kindness. This can align with personal values of compassion and empathy, fostering satisfaction and positive emotional experiences.

4. **Empathy Practice:** Exercising empathy, try to understand the perspective of others. This can improve your ability to connect with others at a deeper level and promote more relevant and meaningful interactions.

Through these practices, the Law of Relevance can be actively incorporated into daily life. As a result, one can cultivate more positive emotional experiences, deter the escalation of negative emotions, and ensure their actions and relationships align with their personal values and priorities.

"Change is the only constant in life." - Heraclitus

THE LAW OF CHANGE

"Therefore, if anyone is in Christ, the new creation has come: The old has gone, the new is here!" - 2 Corinthians 5:17 (NIV)

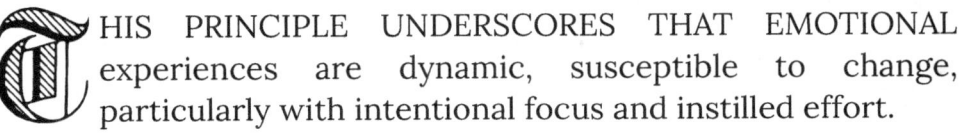 HIS PRINCIPLE UNDERSCORES THAT EMOTIONAL experiences are dynamic, susceptible to change, particularly with intentional focus and instilled effort.

The law recognizes change as an integral part of existence, emphasizing the need for adaptability and resilience for the cultivation of positive emotional experiences and prevention of negative emotions.

Resistance to change or clinging to the past often paves a path towards negative emotions like anxiety, fear, and sadness. In contrast, when we perceive change as an opportunity for growth and adaptation, the probability to experience positive emotions like joy, love, and gratitude multiplies.

Nurturing positive emotional experiences necessitates openness towards change and seeking opportunities for personal growth and evolution. This could involve embracing novel experiences, pursuing fresh goals or interests, or identifying opportunities for personal or professional advancement.

Mindset and beliefs have a powerful impact on our responses to change. Thus, cultivating a growth mindset and a strong belief in our ability to adapt and evolve can help us approach change with optimism and sturdy resilience.

In practical terms, this might involve engaging in regular self-reflection, recognizing areas of life where resistance to change might persist. It could also involve seeking support from mental health professionals or loved ones when increased negative emotions make them challenge to process.

By honoring the Law of Change, we can foster adaptability and resilience, inhibiting the escalation of negative emotions. Remember, embracing change as an opportunity for growth and development can help cultivate positive emotional experiences and boost overall emotional well-being. Change is a constant part of life.

A STORY FROM GRACE'S GARDEN: THE LAW OF CHANGE

Aunt Grace's garden, with its ever-changing scenery through the seasons, was the perfect setting for imparting lessons on self-management, particularly the Law of Change. She often compared the garden's evolution to the dynamic aspect of our emotional experiences.

One breezy afternoon, Grace was joined by her friend Laura, who echoed her struggle with an impending move. Sensing Laura's discomfort, Grace decided to illuminate the law using her garden as a metaphor.

"Laura, dear," she began gently, her eyes surveying over her thriving garden, "Consider this garden. As seasons pass, it undergoes change – the trees shed their leaves in autumn, flowers bloom in spring. However, each change brings a new form of beauty, doesn't it?"

"The garden aligns with the Law of Change, which you can see play out emotionally. Changes, even those seeming daunting, pave the way for growth and new experiences. It's natural to experience anxiety or fear like you're feeling now about the move. But remember, embracing change can lead to positive emotions too." Grace shared her insight.

"Consider this move an opportunity for growth. Seek out the new experiences it might bring, the new relationships you might form. Be open to change as an integral part of life, and nurture that adaptability." Grace finished; her eyes gleaming with understanding.

Amidst the evolving beauty of her garden, Aunt Grace unfolded the essence of the Law of Change to Laura. As Laura listened, she gradually embraced the idea of change, seeing it as an opportunity rather than a hurdle. That afternoon, Grace's wisdom imparted more than just words; it instilled in Laura the resilience to navigate the waves of change with grace and optimism.

CHAPTER SUMMARY

The chapter underscores the Law of Change by reflecting on 2 Corinthians 5:17 (NIV), "Therefore, if anyone is in Christ, the new creation has come: The old has gone, the new is here!" The law emphasizes that emotional experiences, far from being static, are dynamic and can alter with focused, intentional effort.

The inherent constant of life is change, and the Law of Change stresses the importance of being adaptable and resilient. This adaptability helps cultivate positive emotional experiences and curb the control of negative emotions.

Resisting change or holding onto the past can increase the likelihood of experiencing negative emotions like anxiety, fear, and sadness. Conversely, embracing change as an opportunity for growth and adaptation paves the way to positive emotions like joy, love, and gratitude.

For fostering positive emotional experiences, it's crucial to be open to change and seek opportunities for personal growth and evolution. This could include embracing new experiences, pursuing new interests, or identifying opportunities for personal and professional advancement.

One's mindset and beliefs significantly influence the responses to change. Cultivating a growth mindset and firm belief in our ability to adapt and grow allows us to face change with resilience and optimism.

Practically, this may involve regular self-reflection, identifying areas of life where there might be resistance to change, or seeking support from mental health professionals or trusted ones when handling negative emotions becomes overwhelming.

By respecting the Law of Change, we can foster a sense of adaptability and resilience and curb the escalation of negative emotions. Embracing change as a constant part of life, and as an opportunity for growth and development, we can foster positive emotional experiences and enhance emotional well-being.

APPLICATION

Using newly acquired knowledge is an integral component of personal and professional growth. Merely amassing knowledge isn't sufficient; its practical implementation is crucial for tangible results and progress toward individual goals. By translating this knowledge into action, one can improve their skills, boost confidence, and progressively move closer to success.

To effectively implement the Law of Change in a practical context:

1. **Embrace Change:** Be open to change and try to venture into something new or different. This can provide fresh perspectives and possible personal growth.

2. **Flexibility in Life:** Practice flexibility and adaptability in your daily life. An adaptable mindset is key to coping with changes and managing emotional well-being.

3. **New Experiences:** Once again, embrace change and be willing to try new tasks or go down different paths. These can bring fresh experiences, meeting new people, and learning new skills.

4. **Everyday Adaptability:** Reinforce adaptability in your day-to-day life again, as resilient individuals often experience more overall contentment and better handle life's ups and downs.

5. **Step Out of Comfort Zone:** Take calculated risks and step out of your comfort zone. This can foster growth and enhance emotional experiences.

Through these practices, we can better apply the Law of Change actively in daily life. Doing so allows for the cultivation of adaptability and resilience, fostering strong, confident navigation through life's inevitable changes.

"Change is the law of life. And those who look only to the past or present are certain to miss the future." - John F. Kennedy

REFLECTION & GROWTH

"Do not conform to the pattern of this world but be transformed by the renewing of your mind. Then you will be able to test and approve what God's will is—his good, pleasing and perfect will." - Romans 12:2 (NIV)

"When we love, we always strive to become better than we are. When we strive to become better than we are, everything around us becomes better too." - Paulo Coelho

THE LAW OF EXPECTATIONS

"For I know the plans I have for you," declares the Lord, "plans to prosper you and not to harm you, plans to give you hope and a future." - Jeremiah 29:11 (NIV)

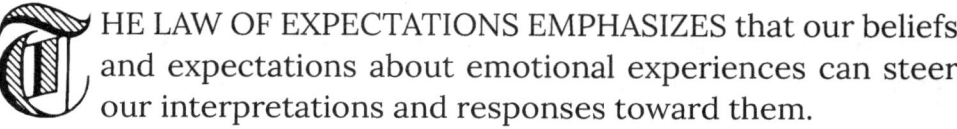

HE LAW OF EXPECTATIONS EMPHASIZES that our beliefs and expectations about emotional experiences can steer our interpretations and responses toward them.

Our emotional experiences are often molded by our expectations. The law highlights the importance of clarity and intentionality about our expectations for fostering positive emotional experiences and preventing negative emotions from burgeoning.

Negative expectations or self-beliefs can exacerbate negative emotions like anxiety, fear, and sadness. On the flip side, positive expectations or beliefs foster positive emotions such as joy, love, and gratitude.

Promoting positive emotional experiences involves being intentional about our expectations and beliefs. These could involve practices such as cognitive-behavioral therapy, reframing negative thought patterns, and actively seeking opportunities to foster positive expectations and beliefs.

Understanding the impact of our expectations on our emotional experiences is crucial. By setting realistic and positive expectations, we can foster a sense of self-confidence, and fulfillment, and prevent negative emotions from escalating.

In a practical lens, this may involve regular self-reflection, and identifying negative thought patterns or beliefs contributing to negative emotional experiences. It could also involve seeking support from mental health professionals or loved ones when handling negative emotions becomes overwhelming.

By respecting the Law of Expectations, we can foster a fulfilling emotional life filled with positivity. It's paramount to remember that our emotional experiences are often shaped by our expectations. By being intentional about these expectations, we can cultivate positive emotional experiences and contain the escalation of negative emotions.

A STORY FROM GRACE'S KITCHEN: THE LAW OF EXPECTATIONS

Warm, vibrant, and filled with the aroma of delicacies brewing, Aunt Grace's kitchen was the ideal spot for conversations about self-awareness, including the Law of Expectations.

One sunny afternoon, Grace noticed her nephew, Ben, looking demoralized as he attempted a new recipe, things not going as he hoped. Although a patient boy, Ben's failed baking attempts were shaking his confidence, making him believe he'd never be good at it. Right then, Grace saw an opportunity to teach him about the Law of Expectations.

"Ben, love," she began, picking up a whisk, "Baking is a lot like managing your expectations. If you start with the belief that you'll fail, more often than not, that's what might happen." She pointed at the egg whites she was whisking, "See these? If I start whisking, thinking they won't stiffen, my energy transmits into my work, and they might not form peaks."

"That's the Law of Expectations at work. Your emotional experiences are quite often shaped by what you expect them to be. If you expect to fail, your anxiety may increase. If you trust in your ability, even if you face a hitch, you'll feel content knowing you gave it your all." Grace explained.

"Don't frame failure as the end. Embrace it as an opportunity for learning and growth. Be open to change and allow some wiggle-room for defects." She finished, sharing an encouraging smile with Ben.

In the comforting heart of Grace's kitchen, the Law of Expectations took shape in a practical lesson. As Ben absorbed her words, he applied them to his next baking attempt. Mixing ingredients with newfound assurance, he savored the process, irrespective of the result. That afternoon, Grace had served up more than just fresh bread. She gifted Ben a critical lesson in managing his expectations and embracing growth, setting the stage for a more confident, optimistic perspective.

CHAPTER SUMMARY

The Law of Expectations, as reflected in Jeremiah 29:11 (NIV), "For I know the plans I have for you," declares the Lord, "plans to prosper you and not to harm you, plans to give you hope and a future," underlines that our anticipations and beliefs about emotional experiences can significantly impact how we perceive and respond to them.

Our emotional experiences frequently shape our expectations. This law underscores the significance of being intentional about our expectations for nurturing positive emotional experiences and preventing the growth of negative emotions.

Negative expectations or beliefs about ourselves or our experiences often translate to negative emotions such as anxiety, fear, and sadness. Conversely, positive expectations or beliefs open the door to positive emotions like joy, love, and gratitude.

Promoting positive emotional experiences involves being intentional about our expectations and beliefs. This could involve participating in cognitive-behavioral therapy, reframing negative thought patterns, and deliberately seeking opportunities to foster positive expectations and beliefs.

Awareness of the influence our expectations can exert over our emotional experiences is also critical. By setting realistic and optimistic expectations for ourselves and our experiences, we contribute to the cultivation of confidence, fulfillment, and the prevention of negative emotion escalation.

In practice, this might involve engaging in regular self-reflection, identifying negative thought patterns or beliefs influencing negative emotional experiences. It might also involve reaching out to mental health professionals or loved ones for support when dealing with overwhelming negative emotions.

By respecting the Law of Expectations, a positive and fulfilling emotional life can take shape. Remembering that our emotional experiences often take shape around our expectations implores us to be intentional about them. Consequently, we can foster positive emotional experiences and curb the escalation of negative emotions.

APPLICATION

Actively applying the knowledge, one gains is a fundamental factor in personal and professional growth. Simply gathering knowledge isn't enough; it should be implemented pragmatically to bring about tangible results and progress toward one's defined goals. By translating new knowledge into action, one can enhance their skills, boost confidence levels, and progressively move closer to success.

To pragmatically apply the Law of Expectations:

1. **Set Realistic Goals:** Establish realistic goals and break them down into manageable, achievable steps. Incremental progression can encourage growth and mitigate feelings of overwhelm or failure.

2. **Self-Compassion:** Practice self-compassion and forgive yourself if you fail to meet your expectations. Everyone faces setbacks, but they're often steppingstones to grander success.

3. **More Compassion:** Double down on practicing self-compassion. Remember, emotional wellbeing thrives on understanding and forgiving oneself when expectations aren't met.

4. **Goal Setting Again:** Reiterate setting realistic goals and chopping them into manageable parts. Repetition and reinforcement of this practice can build up resilience and a positive mindset.

5. **Celebrate Progress:** Recognize and celebrate your progress, no matter how minor it may seem. Each little achievement is a milestone on your larger journey, and they deserve recognition.

By engaging in these practices, we can effectively apply the Law of Expectations in real-life settings. The result is an enhanced sense of confidence, improved emotional wellbeing, and progress toward successfully achieving personal and professional goals.

"We cannot change what we are not aware of, and once we are aware, we cannot help but change." - Sheryl Sandberg

THE LAW OF PROCESSING

"Finally, brothers and sisters, whatever is true, whatever is noble, whatever is right, whatever is pure, whatever is lovely, whatever is admirable—if anything is excellent or praiseworthy—think about such things."
- Philippians 4:8 (NIV)

EARTWORK, THE COGNITIVE AND EMOTIONAL effort needed to understand our experiences, captures the essence of the Law of Processing, as reflected in Philippians 4:8 (NIV), "Finally, brothers and sisters, whatever is true, whatever is noble, whatever is right, whatever is pure, whatever is lovely, whatever is admirable—if anything is excellent or praiseworthy—think about such things."

Emotional processing involves identifying, labeling, and expressing emotions in a healthy and productive way. Emotions are complex and multifaceted, and this law emphasizes the need to dedicate time to comprehend and understand these experiences to foster emotional wellness and cultivate positive emotional experiences.

Failing to allow sufficient time to process our emotional experiences may lead to negative consequences, including increased stress, challenges in regulating emotions, and diminished emotional well-being. In contrast, allotting time to process our emotional experiences can foster a deeper self-understanding, enlightening our emotional responses, and laying the groundwork for better emotional well-being.

Honoring the Law of Processing signals being intentional about reflecting on and understanding emotional experiences. This could involve practices like journaling, mindfulness, meditation, and when necessary, seeking support from mental health professionals or loved ones.

It's also vital to understand the impact of past experiences and traumas on our emotional responses and the necessity to address and process these experiences in a healthy and constructive manner. This can help prevent the escalation of negative emotions, foster positivity, and enhance emotional well-being.

Practically, this might involve regular self-reflection, dedicating time to process and comprehend our emotional experiences, and seeking support when necessary.

By respecting the Law of Processing, we can cultivate a deeper understanding of our emotional responses and lay ground for improved emotional well-being. Remember, emotions are complex. The deliberate process of understanding them is an important step towards nurturing a positive and fulfilling emotional life, preventing negative emotions from gaining a stronghold, and fostering a sense of emotional well-being and fulfillment.

A STORY FROM GRACE'S KITCHEN: THE LAW OF PROCESSING

The aromas, colors, and rhythms of Aunt Grace's kitchen were always the ideal setting for discussions about self-awareness, including the Law of Processing.

One day, Grace's niece, Lily, was visiting. Lily was going through a challenging breakup and seemed lost in a torrent of feelings she couldn't understand. Grace, noticing Lily's distress, invited her to prepare the family's traditional soup together, a task that required patience and meticulousness—much like processing emotions.

"Lily," Grace started, seasoning the broth gently, "See, preparing this soup is a lot like our emotional experiences. Each ingredient, each step is different and requires precise attention. You can't rush the process or skip a step. That might ruin the soup."

"Our emotions demand the same attention. They are multi-layered experiences that need time to understand and process. It isn't easy, but it's important." Grace added the vegetables to the broth, turning down the heat to let it simmer quietly, mirroring the patience needed when dealing with complex emotions.

"In times like yours, when emotions run high, honoring the Law of Processing can help. Take time to identify, label, and express your feelings. You might use a journal or talk to someone trustworthy about them. By doing so, you begin to see patterns and learn valuable insights about yourself." Grace stated calmly, putting a comforting hand over Lily's.

"And remember, it's okay to seek help from professionals to navigate this emotional journey. There's strength in asking for support." Grace added, looking up at Lily with gentle assurance.

In the warm familiarity of Grace's kitchen, amidst simmering soup and stirring spoons, the Law of Processing came to life. Lily found solace in Grace's words, gaining a new understanding of her emotional turmoil. That day, they prepared more than just soup; Grace imparted to Lily a life lesson about the importance of processing emotions, a recipe for emotional well-being she'd carry with her always.

CHAPTER SUMMARY

The Law of Processing, resonating with Philippians 4:8 (NIV), "Finally, brothers and sisters, whatever is true, whatever is noble, whatever is right, whatever is pure, whatever is lovely, whatever is admirable—if anything is excellent or praiseworthy—think about such things," emphasizes the cognitive and emotional efforts that contribute to comprehending our experiences.

The process involves identifying, labeling, and expressing emotions in a healthy and constructive manner. Recognizing the complexity and multifaceted nature of emotions, the Law of Processing highlights that understanding our emotional experiences requires time and intentional efforts—key for promoting emotional wellbeing and cultivating positive emotional experiences.

Not investing sufficient time to process our emotions can lead to negative consequences, including heightened stress, difficulty in regulating emotions, and reduced emotional well-being. Conversely, dedicating time to comprehend emotional experiences enriches our understanding, enhancing emotional well-being.

The Law of Processing necessitates that we intentionally reserve time to process our emotional experiences. The approach might include practices such as journaling, mindfulness, and meditation, or seeking support from mental health professionals or loved ones when necessary.

Awareness of how past experiences and traumas affect our emotional responses is significant, as is the need to process these experiences in a healthy and constructive way. This helps curb the influence of negative emotions and serves to improve emotional well-being.

The practical application of this law might involve regular self-reflection, recognizing and comprehending our emotional experiences, and seeking support when necessary.

The Law of Processing allows for an enriched understanding of emotional experiences and supports improved emotional well-being. Remember, acknowledging complexity in our emotions is an important step toward fostering a positive and fulfilling emotional life. Being intentional about processing our emotional experiences can prevent negative emotions from escalating and promotes emotional well-being and fulfillment.

APPLICATION

Utilizing the knowledge learned is crucial for both personal and professional growth. Merely gaining knowledge isn't sufficient—it needs to be translated into practical applications for tangible results and progress toward one's chosen goals. By transposing newly acquired knowledge into personal action, individuals can augment their skills, bolster confidence, and stride closer to success.

Here's how to practically apply the Law of Processing:

1. **Journaling:** Start keeping a journal. Commit your thoughts and feelings to paper—it helps provide clarity and closure over different emotional experiences.

2. **Self-Reflection:** Regularly engage in the practice of self-reflection. Strive to understand your emotions on a deeper level—it's a core part of emotional processing and growth.

3. **Consistent Journaling:** Emphasize again on maintaining a daily journal. It will help track your emotional patterns and changes over time, providing insights for growth and improvement.

4. **Deeper Understanding:** Reiterate your self-reflection practice, diving deeper into understanding your emotions. Understanding is the first step towards managing emotional well-being effectively.

5. **Seek Support:** If processing difficult emotions, don't hesitate to seek assistance from a competent therapist or a trusted friend. External support can provide fresh perspectives and guidance.

Through these applications, we can effectively integrate the Law of Processing into our daily lives. This not only cultivates a better understanding of our own emotions but also lays the groundwork for improved emotional well-being and fulfillment.

"Your beliefs become your thoughts, your thoughts become your words, your words become your actions, your actions become your habits, your habits become your values, your values become your destiny." - Mahatma Gandhi

THE LAW OF VALIDITY

"Do not conform to the pattern of this world but be transformed by the renewing of your mind. Then you will be able to test and approve what God's will is—his good, pleasing and perfect will." - Romans 12:2 (NIV)

THE ESSENCE OF THE LAW of Validity, captured in Romans 12:2 (NIV) advocates that all emotional experiences are legitimate and tangible, regardless of their perception or reception by others.

We should not only validate our emotional experiences but should also extend respect and acknowledgment to the emotional experiences of others. Our emotional experiences are often shaped around the perceived validity of these experiences. This law underscores the importance of intentional interpretation of our experiences to foster positive emotional experiences and control the rise of negative emotions.

Recognizing our experiences as valid and significant often paves the way to positive emotions such as joy, love, and gratitude. In contrast, perceiving experiences as invalid or insignificant can induce negative emotions like anxiety, fear, and sadness.

Promoting positive emotional experiences requires cognizant interpretation of our experiences and seeking opportunities to discover meaning and purpose. Activities promoting personal growth or emotional fulfillment, like pursuing hobbies, volunteering, or spending quality time with loved ones, can help here.

It's crucial to be aware of how our thoughts and beliefs can impact our interpretation of experiences. Encouraging positive thoughts and beliefs can shift the balance towards positive emotional experiences and hinder the growth of negative emotions.

Practically, this could mean engaging in regular self-reflection, identifying negative thought patterns or beliefs that might amplify negative emotional experiences, and seeking support when these emotions feel overwhelming or difficult to navigate.

By respecting the Law of Validity, we can cultivate a fulfilling emotional life filled with positivity. Remember, our emotional experiences are often shaped around the perceived validity of our experiences. By being intentional about interpreting these experiences, we can foster positive emotional experiences and prevent negative emotions from taking control.

A STORY FROM GRACE'S PORCH: THE LAW OF VALIDITY

Aunt Grace's porch was a serene spot for deep conversations on empathy and social awareness. The quiet buzz of surrounding nature made it the perfect place to discuss the Law of Validity.

One evening, a somber-looking neighboring boy, Tom, stopped by. He had recently lost his dog and felt embarrassed about his deep grief, as people told him it was "just a pet." Sensing his distress, Grace decided to help him understand his emotions better and invited him onto the porch.

"Tom," Grace began her voice steady and soothing, "Emotions, no matter how they might seem to others, are very real and completely valid for the person experiencing them. No one has the right to invalidate them."

"Your grief over your pet is genuine; trivializing it because some might see it as 'just a pet' isn't fair or healthy. That's the Law of Validity at play. Our emotional experiences frame around how valid we perceive them to be," Grace explained, offering the boy a comforting smile.

"Don't suppress your grief because others see it as insignificant. Acknowledge it. Deal with it at your own pace and way. Remember, validation of emotions doesn't require external approval but internal acceptance." Grace finished, handing Tom a warm cup of cocoa.

In the gentle warmth of Grace's porch under the vast evening sky, the Law of Validity gained a new life. As Tom sipped his cocoa, he cocooned into the comfort of Grace's words, finding the courage to accept and deal with his grief without the burden of others' expectations. That evening not only had Grace instilled an important life lesson in Tom, but she also planted the seed of resilience and self-acceptance in him, one that would bloom in the times to come.

CHAPTER SUMMARY

The Law of Validity, reflected in Romans 12:2 (NIV), "Do not conform to the pattern of this world, but be transformed by the renewing of your mind. Then you will be able to test and approve what God's will is—his good, pleasing, and perfect will," highlights that all emotional experiences are real and valid, regardless of how they may be perceived or received by others.

It's important not only to validate our emotions but also to respect and acknowledge others' emotional experiences. Our feelings are often shaped by recognized validity, and the law spotlights the need to be intentional in interpreting our experiences to nurture positivity and prevent negativity.

Seeing our experiences as valid and meaningful tends to evoke positive emotions like joy, love, and gratitude. Conversely, viewing them as invalid or pointless leads to negative emotions such as anxiety, fear, and sadness.

Promoting positive emotional experiences demands intentional interpretation of our experiences and seeking opportunities that impart meaning and purpose. It involves engaging in activities promoting personal growth, emotional fulfillment, and seeking support when required.

A critical aspect is understanding how our thoughts and beliefs impact our interpretation of experiences. Cultivating positive thoughts and beliefs can shift the balance towards positive emotional experiences while hindering the onset of negative emotions.

Practical application of this law involves engaging in regular self-reflection, identifying negative thought patterns or beliefs amplifying negative emotions, and actively seeking support during challenging times.

By honoring the Law of Validity, we cultivate a fulfilling emotional life filled with positivity. Remembering that our emotional experiences often shape around perceived validity is a valuable insight. By being intentional about interpreting these experiences, we can foster positive emotional experiences and prevent the escalation of negative emotions.

APPLICATION

Actively implementing the knowledge, one has learned is a vital element for personal and professional growth. Amassing knowledge isn't enough—it needs to come into practical play for tangible results and progress toward one's self-defined goals. By translating newfound knowledge into action, individuals can further their skills, boost confidence, and steadily move toward success.

Applying the Law of Validity practically requires:

1. **Self-Acceptance:** Embrace your strengths and weaknesses. Loving and accepting yourself as you are forming the basis of validating your own emotional experiences.

2. **Align with Values:** Write down your core values and set an intention to live in harmony with them. Knowing your values can help validate your emotions and decisions aligning with those values.

3. **Repeat Self-Acceptance:** Repeat the practice of self-acceptance. Embracing your virtues and faults aids in accepting the validity of your emotions.

4. **Supportive Surroundings:** Surround yourself with people who understand, accept, and appreciate you as you are. Their acceptance can help in validating your emotions.

5. **Positive Affirmations:** Reframe any negative self-talk and practice positive affirmations. Affirming positivity fosters a more positive mindset, further validating positive emotional experiences.

By implementing these steps, not only do we effectively apply the Law of Validity in our daily life, but we also create an environment to better understand, validate, and manage our emotional experiences, leading to enhanced self-awareness and overall emotional well-being.

"Always be yourself, express yourself, have faith in yourself, do not go out and look for a successful personality and duplicate it." - Bruce Lee

THE LAW OF PERSONALITY

"So, God created mankind in his own image, in the image of God he created them; male and female he created them." - Genesis 1:27 (NIV)

THE LAW OF PERSONALITY, AS mirrored in Genesis 1:27, accentuates that our individual personality traits can significantly influence our emotional experiences and expression mode.

Recognizing and accepting our unique emotional style can pave the way towards healthy emotional experiences and relationships. Our emotional experiences are deeply tied to our unique personalities. This law underpins the importance of remaining faithful to our authentic selves in order to foster positivity and prevent the rise of negative emotions.

When we project a version of ourselves disconnected from our true nature or suppress aspects of our real personalities, we invite negative emotions such as anxiety, fear, and sadness. On the contrary, embracing and expressing our authentic selves can lead to positive emotions like joy, love, and gratitude.

Creating positive emotional experiences involves staying true to ourselves and seeking opportunities that celebrate our authentic selves. This might encompass activities that resonate with our values and interests, finding supportive communities, or seeking growth opportunities complementing our unique personalities.

It's crucial to recognize the impact of societal expectations and norms on our self-images and emotional experiences. Challenging societal expectations misaligned with our authentic nature helps in nurturing self-acceptance, self-love, and curbing negative emotions.

Practically, this could involve regular self-reflection, identifying aspects of our personality we might suppress or ignore, and seeking support when negative emotions seem unmanageable.

By honoring the Law of Personality, we cultivate a deeper sense of self-acceptance and self-love, curbing the stronghold of negative emotions. Remembering our emotional experiences are deeply connected to our unique personalities is vital. By staying true to our authentic selves, we can foster positive emotional experiences and improved emotional well-being.

A Story from Grace's Garden: The Law of Personality

Aunt Grace's garden, a symphony of colors and fragrances, was an apt setting for lessons about self-management. This particular afternoon, the lesson was regarding the Law of Personality.

Her grandchild, Ethan, was struggling with his decisive nature. At school, his peers often misinterpreted his clarity as dominating. Intimidated by these judgments, Ethan had started to suppress this quality, leading him to feel inauthentic and anxious.

Sensing Ethan's struggle, Grace invited him to help in her rose garden, a place where diverse personalities of different blossoms coexisted beautifully—just the right metaphor she needed.

"Ethan," she began, tending to a vigorous climber, "See this rose here? Some people might find it too bold, trying to reach for the stars. Others might admire its ambition. But regardless of these perspectives, it doesn't change its nature; it grows in its authentic way, just like our personalities."

"There's a law called the Law of Personality. It implies that our true nature influences our emotions. The more we embrace it, the more positive our emotional world becomes." she explained, plucking a rose bloom, "But if we deny our authenticity, suppress who we are, we invite negative feelings like anxiety and distress."

"You're a decisive person, and that's a wonderful trait. Don't dampen it due to others' misconceptions. Celebrate your qualities, Ethan. Be proud of who you are." Grace finished, handing the freshly plucked rose to Ethan.

There, among the colorful blooms and scents of Grace's garden, the Law of Personality unfolded as potently as the aromas of the roses. Ethan, with fresh understanding, decided to accept his decisiveness, his rose, in all its uniqueness—embrace his personality rather than disguise it. His looming distress began to ease. In Grace's nurturing garden, not only did flowers bloom, but young Ethan did as well.

CHAPTER SUMMARY

Underlying the Law of Personality, as reflected in Genesis 1:27 (NIV): "So God created mankind in his own image, in the image of God he created them; male and female he created them," is the understanding that our individual personality traits significantly influence our emotional experiences and expressiveness.

It's important to recognize and affirm our unique emotional style, as it paves the way to nurturing healthier emotional experiences and relationships. Our emotional experiences are profoundly influenced by our distinct personalities, underlining the importance of staying true to our authentic selves. This approach cultivates positive emotions and curbs the rise of negative ones.

Trying to suppress our true nature or projecting a dishonest version of ourselves often leads to negative emotions, like anxiety, fear, and sadness. In contrast, when we embrace and express our authenticity, we're more likely to experience positive emotions, such as joy, love, and gratitude.

Generating positive emotional experiences involves being true to our authentic selves and seeking opportunities that celebrate this authenticity. This might involve activities resonating with our values and interests, finding supportive communities, or pursuing growth opportunities that align with our unique personalities.

Societal expectations and norms can deeply impact our personal and emotional experiences. It's crucial to challenge these societal expectations when they don't align with our authenticity, fostering self-acceptance, self-love and controlling negative emotions.

Practical application of this law can involve regular self-reflection, identifying aspects of our personality that we may suppress, and seeking support when negative emotions seem overwhelming.

By honoring the Law of Personality, we can cultivate a profound sense of self-acceptance and self-love, which can keep negative emotions at bay. Remembering that our emotional experiences are intimately tied to our unique personalities, we can remain authentic and foster positive emotional experiences and enhanced emotional wellness.

APPLICATION

Inculcating the knowledge, one has gathered is a crucial factor for personal and professional growth. Merely amassing knowledge isn't sufficient—it needs to be implemented pragmatically to yield palpable results and progress toward achieving one's goals. By transmuting fresh knowledge into action, individuals can advance their skills, enhance confidence, and edge closer to success.

To practically employ the Law of Personality in your life:

1. **Self-Compassion and Love:** Practice self-compassion and self-love and learn to appreciate your unique personality traits. Every personality is unique and brings something special to the table.

2. **Embrace Authenticity:** Set an intention to live authentically and to embrace your true self. Living authentically can lead to a more fulfilling life and positive emotional well-being.

3. **Repeat Self-Love & Compassion:** Again, practice self-love and self-compassion, and learn to value your unique personality traits. Embracing your unique traits can help mitigate negative emotional experiences.

4. **Seek Happiness:** Reflect on the activities that spark joy for you and prioritize them in your life. This aids in aligning with your true self and promotes better emotional wellness.

5. **Practice Authenticity:** Insist on authenticity and strive to live in alignment with your true self. Authentic living leads to the

validation of your emotional experiences, fostering positivity and combating negativity.

By adopting these practices, we tangibly apply the Law of Personality into routine life, fostering a healthier emotional landscape, accelerating personal growth, and nurturing a deep sense of self-love and acceptance.

"Life is a journey, and if you fall in love with the journey, you will be in love forever." - Peter Hagerty

EMBRACING THE JOURNEY

"May the God of hope fill you with all joy and peace as you trust in him, so that you may overflow with hope by the power of the Holy Spirit." - Romans 15:13 (NIV)

"But the fruit of the Spirit is love, joy, peace, forbearance, kindness, goodness, faithfulness, gentleness, and self-control. Against such things there is no law." - Galatians 5:22-23 (NIV)

"Finally, all of you, be like-minded, be sympathetic, love one another, be compassionate and humble." - 1 Peter 3:8 (NIV)

THE JOURNEY EMBRACED: REFLECTING ON THE LAWS OF HEARTFELT EMOTIONS

AS WE CONCLUDE OUR EXPLORATION of the 16 Laws of Heartfelt Emotions, let us remember that emotional wellbeing is not a destination—it's an ongoing, ever-evolving journey. The 16 Laws we've explored serve as a compass to guide us on this journey.

Every journey comes with its own set of challenges and victories. The road toward emotional wellbeing is no different and understanding the pros and cons involved can better equip us for the adventure.

Pros:

By honoring each of these laws, we are able to:

- Gain greater self-awareness and understanding of our emotions and those of others.

- Develop emotional resilience and respond to emotional challenges efficiently.

- Foster healthier and more harmonious relationships

- Promote mental health and overall wellbeing.

- Influence the world around us positively through better emotional management.

Cons:

However, it's important to recognize potential challenges:

- The journey can involve confronting and processing uncomfortable emotions.

- Misinterpretation or misuse of the laws could potentially lead to emotional avoidance.

- Progress may seem slow or sporadic and require patience.

- Regular self-reflection and introspection may be time-consuming.

- Overemphasis on one law while neglecting others could disrupt emotional balance.

As you progress on your quest towards emotional wellbeing, always remember to be kind and patient with yourself. Emotions can be brimming with complexity—it's okay to encounter struggles. The commitment to continue—the unbarring pursuit of growth, learning, and healing—is truly what matters.

It is my heartfelt hope that "The 16 Laws of Heartfelt Emotions" has served as a roadmap for this journey, empowering you to cultivate enhanced emotional wellbeing in your life. Embrace your uniqueness, prioritize your wellbeing, and remain open to change and growth. By honoring these 16 Laws, we can not only nurture a positive and fulfilling emotional life within ourselves but also contribute to a more emotionally healthy and empathetic world for everyone.

Thank you for joining me on this journey—here's to a future brimming with love, joy, and gratitude in your emotional life. Together we can weather setbacks and continue to grow, coloring the world with the hues of emotional maturity and wellbeing.

A STORY FROM GRACE'S KITCHEN: EMBRACING THE JOURNEY - SELF-AWARENESS

Aunt Grace's kitchen was rich with the fragrant smell of baked apple pie, a smell that immediately warmed the heart of anyone who entered. The kitchen was the perfect place for lifetimes of lessons about self-awareness.

Today, Grace's granddaughter, Lily, visited. Lately, Lily was struggling at school with her perfectionism, pressuring herself to excel in every area and beating herself up when she didn't. Recognizing the teachable moment, Grace decided to use their baking activity to illustrate an important lesson -- embracing the journey.

As Lily stepped into the kitchen, Grace invited her to help with the apple pie, "You know, Lily," Grace said, stirring the filling, "a perfect apple pie isn't about having every slice of apple identical or each sprinkle of cinnamon exact."

With a soft reassurance in her voice, she continued, "The magic lies in understanding and accepting how each component plays a unique part in creating this beautiful dessert. It's a journey—from choosing the right apples, to accepting their natural shape, to folding them within this handmade crust."

In this bubbling kitchen, the apple pie served as Grace's analogy for the journey of self-awareness—a journey of understanding and accepting one's strengths, weaknesses, and unique personality traits.

Similarly, Lily needed to embrace her journey,—her strengths, her weaknesses, her ambitions—with patience and self-kindness, understanding that everyone has their own pace, their own set of challenges, and their unique recipe to their personal growth journey. Perfection isn't the goal; it's about progression, about embracing the journey of becoming.

As the scent of the pie filled the kitchen, Lily began to understand the warmth in Grace's words: it wasn't about striving for flawless execution, but about accepting oneself, about seeing the value in one's unique journey of experiencing and growing.

In the heart of that homely kitchen, not only was the perfect apple pie baked that day, but also a young girl started her journey towards true self-awareness, a journey marked not by perfection, but by patient acceptance and self-love. The aroma of the apple pie was forever etched in Lily's heart as a reminder of her grandmother's lifelong lessons.

A STORY FROM GRACE'S GARDEN: EMBRACING THE JOURNEY - SELF-MANAGEMENT

Aunt Grace's garden was a living testament to patience, care, and growth—essentials of self-management. Today's visitor was young Sam, her neighbor's son, who was feeling overwhelmed with his over-packed schedule and struggling with managing his time and commitments.

Sensing his dilemma, Grace invited Sam to help her in the garden. As they began to prune and water the plants, Grace started to share her wisdom, subtly intertwined with garden metaphors.

"Sam," Grace began gently, "A garden can't bloom all at once. Each seed we plant needs its own time, the right amount of water, sunlight—its own space. We can't rush the roses to bloom alongside the daisies; it's about managing what is necessary at its own pace."

Bent over a rose bush, she pruned its overgrown branches, "Overcrowding the garden doesn't make it bloom faster or better. It's the same with our commitments; trying to do everything at once won't necessarily help us achieve our goals any quicker or better. It might, in fact, stress us out."

She gestured around the garden, "Much like this garden, our life needs careful planning, prioritizing, and time management—giving each goal its own space to grow."

Her words hit home. Sam began to see his obstacles in managing school, sports, hobbies, and friendships as akin to Grace's garden—needing careful nurturing, patience, and management. He realized he had over-sown his garden with commitments and that pruning was the need of the hour.

In Grace's nurtured garden, Sam didn't just learn about plants. He discovered the importance of self-management, of prioritization and balance in his commitments. An afternoon in the garden guided him on his journey of understanding that in order to ensure every aspect of his life could grow and flourish in its own time, effective self-management was crucial.

With determination in his mind and relief in his heart, Sam would always remember this lesson, this day in the garden and the wisdom imparted by Aunt Grace.

A Story from Grace's Porch: Embracing the Journey - Social Awareness and Empathy

Aunt Grace's porch, bathed in the soft glow of the setting sun, was the arena for discussions on social awareness and empathy. That evening, her guest was a grumpy neighbor, Mr. Cooper, who recently had a heated interaction with a group of teenagers from the neighborhood.

With refreshing lemonade and her comforting presence, Grace invited a grumbling Mr. Cooper onto the porch. "Now, Mr. Cooper," she eventually began, after offering him a calming moment with the lemonade, "consider the evening sky."

She guided his gaze to the horizon, "You see, much like that horizon, we all have different perspectives, different views on things. It's what makes us unique. Understanding this, and accepting it, is the beginning of social awareness and empathy."

Grace paused and gestured to the glass of lemonade, "It's like this lemonade, some might find it too sour, some too sweet, but that doesn't make it wrong, it just means everyone has different tastes."

She added on, "Empathy is about putting ourselves in another's shoes - imagining what they're going through. The teenagers you argued with, have you thought of their perspective? Maybe they don't even realize the noise could be disruptive. Empathy could help foster dialogue, understanding, and possibly a resolution."

On her porch, under the wide paint-streaked sky, Mr. Cooper found himself softening, his view expanding. He began to realize that he had been so caught up in his own standpoint that he'd overlooked the adolescents' viewpoint. Empathy was a powerful tool, and he'd forgotten to apply it.

Under the expanding colors of the horizon, Aunt Grace's porch was not just a spot for deep conversations, but also turning points. Thanks to Grace's wise words, not only had Mr. Cooper started to assess the situation with a broader perspective, filled with empathy, but also, he began his journey towards becoming more socially aware. In the heartening light of the setting sun, the porch had once again served as Grace's nurturing ground for a vital life lesson.

A Story from Grace's Family Room: Embracing the Journey - Relationships

Aunt Grace's family room was cozy and inviting. Filled with photos, keepsakes, and comfortable furnishings, it was the perfect backdrop for discussions on relationships.

Her nephew, Jack, had been grappling with the end of a friendship. He was finding it difficult to let go, feeling a mix of anger, guilt, and sadness. Sensing his struggle, Grace decided to create an open dialogue about this often complex and challenging part of life.

As Jack stepped into the family room, Grace gestured for him to take a seat next to her, "Jack," Grace started, her eyes warm with understanding. "Look around this room, you see these pictures, mementos, each representing a relationship. Some are still strong, timeless, while others, well, have run their course."

Grace picked up a faded photo of a young her with a friend, a sense of nostalgia passing over her, "Take my old friend Lucy here, we were inseparable growing up, but one day, we realized we were on different paths. It was painful letting go, but embracing the journey of our separate lives was essential."

Grace explained further, "Much like these keepsakes, relationships, too, have lifetimes. Some are forever, while others last only for a season. It's crucial to embrace not only the building but also the fading and letting go of relationships. It's a part of the journey, Jack."

In the nostalgia-filled atmosphere of the family room, Jack started understanding what Grace was unfolding - the journey of relationships. Jack needed to acknowledge the pain, but also understand the necessity of drifting apart and letting go as part of his personal journey.

Jack looked at the fading photo again, and this time, he felt a sense of peace. He realized that like his Aunt Grace, he too could cherish the memories and let go of the pain and guilt.

That evening, in the comfort of Grace's family room, Jack learned that the path to successful relationships is a journey—a voyage of building, maintaining, and sometimes, letting go. Jack understood that embracing both the joys and challenges of relationships was an integral part of his journey, a sentiment he would cherish forever.

CHAPTER SUMMARY

Embracing the journey is integral to the narrative we've been unfolding. Inherently embedded in biblical verses such as Romans 15:13 (NIV), Galatians 5:22-23 (NIV), and 1 Peter 3:8 (NIV), we see the significance of recognizing the ongoing, ever-evolving journey of emotional well-being reflected in our exploration of the 16 Laws of Heartfelt Emotions.

Emotional well-being is neither a quick fix nor a finite goal—it's a lifelong journey. Each of the 16 Laws we've discussed provides guidance, but the journey is always advancing, evolving, and adapting.

An important facet to remember is emotional well-being is not an isolated undertaking. We're all interlinked, with our emotional experiences influenced by our interactions with the world around us. As we foster greater emotional well-being and fulfillment, we can not only impact our own lives positively but also those around us and contribute to overall societal positivity.

Throughout this journey towards enhanced emotional well-being, it's vital to be patient and kind to oneself. Emotions can be complex, and it's perfectly normal to grapple with them at times. Persistence in the exploration, and consistently seeking avenues for growth, learning, and healing, are the most valuable elements of this journey.

"The 16 Laws of HEARTfelt Emotions" aims to serve as a guide, an empowering manuscript to enhance your emotional wellbeing. Embrace your individuality, prioritize your wellbeing, and stay open to growth and adaptation. Honoring the 16 Laws laid out in our course paves the way to cultivating a fulfilling emotional life and contributes to a more caring and aware society for all.

Thank you for being a part of this journey. Lean into your emotional life, fill it with love, joy, and gratitude. Let's together leave imprints of emotional maturity and overall well-being, making the emotional landscape around us a bright, affirming space.

APPLICATION

Incorporating the knowledge, one has accumulated is a critical aspect of personal and professional growth. Simply gaining knowledge isn't enough—it must be deployed in real-life scenarios to achieve tangible results and move closer to one's goals. When we convert new knowledge into action, we can enhance our skills, foster confidence, and proceed toward success.

Here's how to practically adopt the concept of "Embracing the Journey" in your daily life:

1. **Recognize the Journey:** Understand that emotional well-being is an ongoing, lifelong journey rather than a fixed goal. Appreciate every step, whether it involves leaps forward, minor progress, or even temporary setbacks.

2. **Emotional Intelligence:** Regularly practice self-reflection to understand your emotions, thoughts, and behaviors better. Cultivate strategies to manage your emotions effectively and build resilience.

3. **Embrace Individuality:** Celebrate your uniqueness and continuously strive to live authentically. Understand and embrace the influence of your personality on your emotions and reactions.

4. **Compassionate Relationships:** Actively work on building healthy relationships—with others and yourself. Practice empathy, kindness, and open communication.

5. **Continuous Learning:** Foster a mindset of lifelong learning. Seize opportunities for personal growth and deepen your understanding of emotions and emotional well-being.

6. **Embrace Change:** Acknowledge that change is an inevitable part of the journey. Maintain flexibility in your approach and adapt to changes with grace and resilience.

By actively putting into practice these actionable points, we can better navigate the journey of emotional well-being, further fostering personal growth, enhancing resilience, and nurturing a deeper connection with ourselves and others. This practice encapsulates the essence of the journey we have embarked upon while exploring the 16 Laws of Heartfelt Emotions. Remember, it's about progress, not perfection. Embrace your journey.

"The key to life is accepting challenges. Once someone stops doing this, he's dead." – Bette Davis

CRAFTING YOUR ACTION PLAN

"In their hearts humans plan their course, but the LORD establishes their steps." - Proverbs 16:9 (NIV)

"Commit to the LORD whatever you do, and he will establish your plans." - Proverbs 16:3 (NIV)

"May he give you the desire of your heart and make all your plans succeed." - Psalm 20:4 (NIV)

THE SCRIPTURE-GUIDED HEARTFELT EMOTIONS PATHWAY

UPON JOURNEYING THROUGH THE 16 Laws of Heartfelt Emotions, now is the opportune time to translate your insights into an actionable plan. Implementing these newfound principles in your daily life can lead to enhanced emotional well-being, personal growth, healthier relationships, and a profound sense of fulfillment. The Scriptures provide us with wisdom and guidance for this journey.

Let's delve into an actionable plan inspired by the principles of scripture:

1. **Self-awareness:** Dedicate time each day for introspective reflection, as urged in Lamentations 3:40 (NIV), "Let us examine our ways and test them." Understand your emotions, reactions, thoughts, and behaviors through activities such as journaling.

Certify time every day for introspection. Reflect on your emotions, reactions, thoughts, and behaviors. Try journaling as a tool for exploring your feelings and understanding your triggers.

2. **Self-management:** Draw from Proverbs 25:28 (NIV), a fortressed city is one with self-control. Setting healthy boundaries, learning to say no, managing stress, and balancing time can be profound steps in personal growth.

Establish clear boundaries and learn to say no when necessary. Practice stress management techniques such as meditation, exercise, or even gardening. Prioritize time management and balance in your professional and personal life.

3. **Relationship Management:** Lean on the wisdom of Ephesians 4:2 (NIV), be patient, bearing with one another in love. Prioritize honest communication and cultivate meaningful, positive relationships.

Cultivate positive relationships. Communicate openly and honestly and make time for loved ones. Practice empathy and understanding and be patient during disagreements.

4. **Social Awareness and Empathy:** Embrace the teaching in Luke 6:31(NIV), "Do to others as you would have them do to you". Extend your understanding to others, respect diverse perspectives, and show kindness.

Extend your consciousness beyond yourself. Understand and respect diverse perspectives and cultures. Show kindness to strangers and contribute to your community.

5. **Individuality - Remain authentic:** In the words of Psalm 139:14 (NIV), we're wonderfully made. Treasure your uniqueness, stay authentic, and honor your values and beliefs.

—celebrate your unique self without comparing yourself to others. Honor your values, beliefs, and interests consistently.

6. **Intentional Growth:** Proverbs 18:15 teaches us that the heart of the discerning acquires knowledge. Cultivate a lifelong learning mindset, seize growth opportunities, and embrace personal growth.

Adopt an attitude of continuous learning. Read, attend workshops, and take up new hobbies. Embrace the journey of personal growth and realize that it's a lifelong process.

7. **Emotional Wellbeing:** Seek help when needed, as Galatians 6:2 invites us to bear each other's burdens. Tune into your emotional health and celebrate every triumph, no matter how small.

Attune to your emotional health. Seek professional help when needed, just like you would for physical health. Remember to celebrate your progress, no matter how small.

8. **Practice Positivity:** Philippians 4:8(NIV) invites us to dwell on what is true, noble, and right. Engage in gratitude journaling and mindfulness, embrace optimism, and honor all emotions without judgment.

Incorporate positive practices such as gratitude journaling, affirmations, or mindfulness. Embrace optimism yet honor your full spectrum of emotions without judgment.

9. **Health & Wellness:** 1 Corinthians 6:19-20 (NIV) reminds us of the importance of our bodies. Proper nutrition, regular exercise, adequate sleep, and regular check-ups are vital.

Look after your physical health as it impacts your emotional wellbeing. Eat healthily, exercise regularly, get enough sleep, and have regular check-ups.

10. **Continuous Assessment:** Draw inspiration from Proverbs 16:9, where we are reminded how our plans and steps are guided by the Lord. Regularly revisit your goals, assess your emotional wellbeing, and adjust your action plan as required.

Regularly reassess your goals and emotional wellbeing. Adjust your action plan as required to fit any changes in your life. It's your journey—flexibility is key.

Remember, this action plan is your guide— tailor it according to your needs, priorities, and circumstances. Cherish your unique journey at your pace. Make necessary changes, focus on progress rather than perfection, mirroring the wisdom of scriptures in your pathway to embracing a fulfilling emotional life.

In the garden of your heart, cultivate the seeds of peace, nurture the blooms of harmony, and watch as the branches of growth reach toward the heavens. Just as the laws in this book are the gentle winds guiding your emotional garden, may you find serenity in the dance of your own flourishing soul. – Dr. Tracie Hines Lashley

ABOUT THE AUTHOR

"Peace, I leave with you; my peace I give you. I do not give to you as the world gives. Do not let your hearts be troubled and do not be afraid." - John 14:27 (NIV)

"Make every effort to keep the unity of the Spirit through the bond of peace." - Ephesians 4:3 (NIV)

"I am the vine; you are the branches. If you remain in me and I in you, you will bear much fruit; apart from me, you can do nothing." - John 15:5 (NIV)

IN THE TAPESTRY OF MY life, emotions have been the vibrant hues painting stories of joy, resilience, and connection. From the overwhelming joy of cradling my firstborn to the profound sorrow etched in the lines of life's trials, emotions have been my constant companions, shaping the very essence of my journey.

This journey, rife with the complexities of emotions, spurred the creation of "The 16 Laws of HEARTfelt Emotions" — a sincere endeavor to untangle the threads of emotional intelligence and well-being.

Within these pages, you've not just read but experienced the exploration of emotions. From the intimate, individual brushstrokes of our emotional canvas to the symphony of connections shaping our emotional landscape, the book delved into the very core of processing and regulating emotions, the sway of expectations and beliefs, and the profound transformation held within the dance of momentum and change.

Through these 16 Laws, we haven't just uncovered the intricacies of emotions; we've held in our hands practical tools to nurture emotional intelligence and kindle the flame of well-being. Together, we've discovered the profound impact of empathy, compassion, and emotional wellness, not just in our lives but in the tapestry of the world.

In the midst of our intricate world, emotional intelligence and well-being stand as beacons of light. By embracing the 16 Laws of heartfelt emotions, we are crafting a legacy of brightness and compassion, not only for ourselves but for the unfolding generations.

May this book resonate with the depths of your own emotional journey. I'm not just an author; I'm a fellow traveler, eagerly walking alongside you. Let's continue this shared exploration, hand in hand, as we navigate the beautiful tapestry of our emotions and step into the promise of a more connected and compassionate tomorrow.

"Personal growth is not a matter of learning new information but of unlearning old limits." - Alan Cohen

CONTINUED GROWTH

"Being confident of this, that he who began a good work in you will carry it on to completion until the day of Christ Jesus." - Philippians 1:6 (NIV)

A S YOU EMBARK ON THE journey of continued personal growth and emotional well-being, HEARTfelt Intelligence is committed to being your companion on this enriching path. Our dedication extends beyond the pages of this book, aiming to provide ongoing support and resources to foster your development.

PROGRAMS

Explore specialized programs designed to deepen your understanding of emotional intelligence and its practical applications. From workshops that delve into specific laws to immersive experiences promoting self-discovery, our programs cater to various aspects of your personal and emotional growth.

COURSES

Enroll in courses crafted by experts in the field, offering in-depth insights into the 16 Laws of HEARTfelt Emotions. These courses provide a structured learning environment, allowing you to delve into specific areas of interest, reinforce key principles, and apply them in your daily life.

COMMUNITY ENGAGEMENT

Join our vibrant community of like-minded individuals on a similar journey. Engage in discussions, share experiences, and gain valuable insights from a diverse group of individuals who are committed to fostering emotional intelligence and well-being.

MENTORSHIP OPPORTUNITIES

Benefit from personalized guidance through mentorship programs. Connect with experienced mentors who can offer support, share their own journeys, and provide valuable advice as you navigate the intricacies of personal growth.

EXCLUSIVE RESOURCES

Access a wealth of exclusive resources, including articles, podcasts, and additional materials that complement and expand upon the teachings in "The 16 Laws of HEARTfelt Emotions." Stay informed and inspired on your ongoing journey towards emotional intelligence.

At HEARTfelt Intelligence, we believe that personal growth is a continuous and evolving process. We are here to accompany you every step of the way, offering a spectrum of resources and opportunities that align with your unique path to a more emotionally intelligent and fulfilling life.

STANDARD HI-EQ WEBSITE: www.heartfelteiq.com

CHRIST-CENTER WEBSITE: www.kingdomshepherd.com